Super
Ha
GW00362115

Other books by William Davis

Three Years' Hard Labour
Merger Mania
Money Talks
Have Expenses, Will Travel
It's No Sin to be Rich
The Best of Everything (editor)
Money in the 1980s
The Rich: a study of the species
Fantasy: a practical guide to escapism
The Corporate Infighter's Handbook
The World's Best Business Hotels (editor)

The Supersalesman's Handbook

William Davis

Illustrations by John Jensen

ARROW BOOKS

Arrow Books Limited
62–65 Chandos Place, London WC2N 4NW

An imprint of Century Hutchinson Limited

London Melbourne Sydney Auckland
Johannesburg and agencies throughout
the world

First published in Great Britain
by Sidgwick & Jackson Ltd 1986

Arrow edition 1987

Photoset by Rowland Phototypesetting Limited
Bury St Edmunds, Suffolk
Printed and bound in Great Britain by
Anchor Brendon Limited, Tiptree, Essex

ISBN 0 09 949880 4

I am grateful to John Jensen for illustrating the book.

Contents

Introduction

The cliché image of the salesman, much loved by comedians, is that of a wretched figure trudging from door to door in a forlorn bid to sell unwanted brushes and encyclopaedias – and leading, like Willie Loman in Arthur Miller's great play, the *Death of a Salesman*, a life of quiet desperation.

We laugh because he seems so pathetic, and because it feels good to be reminded that *we* don't have to earn our living in such an undignified and soul-destroying manner.

It is a short step from this contemptuous portrait of the 'typical' salesman to the snobbish view (a hangover from the days when people who lived off dividends would sneer at anyone in 'trade') that the whole business of selling deserves to be treated with disdain and condescension.

And yet there is a real sense in which we are *all* selling something – a service, an idea, a philosophy, or just ourselves. Anyone who has ever tried to persuade someone else to accept this argument (and who hasn't?) is a salesman, even though he or she may be reluctant to accept that label, let alone identify with characters like Willie Loman.

The young man who applies for a promising job is selling his main asset: his abilities, whatever they may be.

The lawyer who persuades a client to go into battle over some grievance is selling his legal skills.

The stockbroker who convinces you to buy a block of shares is selling his investment expertise.

The clergyman who urges you to come to Church on Sunday is selling faith.

The politician who seeks your vote is selling his party's brand of idealism – often in the same way as that pathetic door-to-door salesman.

The film star who hawks his services around the studios is selling his good looks and what small talent he may possess.

The TV commentator or newspaper columnist who claims to be disgusted by salesmanship is selling what he never seems to be short of – an opinion.

The comedian who makes fun of salesmen is selling a product which he clearly considers to be superior to brushes and encyclopaedias – his jokes.

Clearly, though, some people are better at it than others. They are the supersalesmen who can swing deals worth millions or change the course of entire countries – sometimes even the course of world history. Lenin was a supersalesman. So was Hitler, who sold his gullible countrymen a quack medicine for the twin ills of unemployment and humiliation.

Modern politics has more than its share of accomplished performers, and elections, especially in America, have increasingly become expensive sales campaigns, with candidates for high office marketed like a new brand of toothpaste or a new car. You don't get to the White House, nowadays, unless you are a supersalesman.

In business the biggest prices often go to the people who know how to sell. It doesn't have to be a product: ideas can produce much bigger returns. Vast fortunes have been made, and continue to be made, through clever salesmanship in the world of finance.

You can start a company and, once it is successful, sell it to a larger group, or to the public through a stock market flotation.

You can dream up a clever real estate deal and sell the

concept to a financial institution; it puts up the funds, you make the money.

You can develop a business and, like McDonald's and Colonel Sanders, sell franchises to others. They do the work, you get a share of the income.

You can buy a stake in another company, threaten to make a take-over bid, and then agree to sell your shares to the frightened board and its supporters at a vast profit.

You can start an investment group, whose sole asset is your expertise, and sell its shares to people who prefer to let others do the thinking for them.

Remember Bernie Cornfeld? He is the salesman who, in the 1960s, made a fortune by exploiting the gullibility – and greed – of small investors by launching his own mutual funds.

A mutual fund is ostensibly an outfit which, for the mutual enrichment of its shareholders, gathers money from them, puts the money into a pool and invests it – most commonly in stocks. If the investments are sound, the pool gets bigger and so does each investor's share. In hustling fund shares to the public, salesmen usually stress two points: 1) that a small investor can command a greater diversity of stocks through fund ownership than he could by buying individual stocks himself and 2) that he gets the advantage of what is portentously called 'professional money management'.

Cornfeld hired a team of salesmen like himself and devised an enticing slogan: 'Do you sincerely want to be rich?' He also came up with a smart new idea: 'A Fund of Funds', which would invest mainly in other mutual funds. He made millions in commissions, management fees and the sale of shares in his master company, IOS.

The whole edifice eventually collapsed when the world's stock markets went into a sharp decline. The value of Cornfeld's dizzy speculations plummeted and many investments were wiped out altogether. No one wanted to buy his fund shares any more; hordes of investors, painfully aware that his promises could not be kept, deserted him.

Cornfeld was a lousy money manager, but no one has ever denied that he was a supersalesman.

So was another entrepreneur who, from humble beginnings, built up an enormous fortune – Ray Kroc. His story is a classic example of the small-time pedlar who gets rich by spotting an opportunity and making the most of it.

Kroc dropped out of school and, for a while, sold real estate in Florida. It was a disaster – he was left disillusioned and broke. He then turned to selling Multimixers – machines that could make a number of milkshakes at one time. In 1954 he discovered that a small restaurant in California, run by Mac and Dick McDonald, had eight of his mixers. No one else had that many, and Kroc decided to see the McDonald operation for himself. The brothers, he found, were doing a roaring trade in hamburgers and milkshakes. When he asked why they didn't open more restaurants (he wanted to sell them more mixers) they said that they were quite content to stick to the one they had. 'If we opened a chain,' Dick McDonald told him, 'I'd never be home.'

Kroc saw his chance and grabbed it. The McDonalds agreed to let him franchise their outlets anywhere in the country in exchange for half a per cent of the gross receipts. He opened his first McDonald's, which he owned himself, in a Chicago suburb the following year and others quickly followed. In 1960 he decided to buy the name McDonald outright for $2.7 million. By the mid-1970s Kroc had franchise holders all over the world and his personal wealth was estimated at $300 million.

Kroc was one of the first to get into the franchise game; many others have done so since. But there are even easier ways to make a fortune. You merely have to know the right people.

Middlemen often collect huge sums by acting as sales agents. Take Adnan Kashoggi, who was the model for the principal character in the best-selling Harold Robbins novel *The Pirate*. His father was a personal physician to King Ibn Saud; it established a royal connection which turned out to be immensely useful when the little desert kingdom began to make all that money from oil. Kashoggi soon had the Saudi agencies for Marconi, Fiat, Chrysler and Rolls-Royce aero-engines. His royal links also got him involved in lucrative arms deals. He was paid a commission of $45 million from the sale of French tanks to the Saudi army and, in the years that followed, earned more than $100 million from Lockheed and another $54 million from its rivals, Northrop. It allowed him to build up a formidable business empire, with operations in thirty-eight countries: banking, property development, hotels, ship chartering, meat packing, insurance, fashion, hospital management and so on.

Not everyone, of course, can be a Ray Kroc or an Adnan Kashoggi. But there is no reason why a competent salesman should settle for being a Willie Loman. In today's world, salesmanship is a major route to success and anyone can join the race. A humble background is not a barrier; nor is a lack of formal education. A woman may find the going a little harder than a man, but there are no rules which prevent her from reaching the top. The basic qualifications are an urge to win, the ability to cope with setbacks and a talent for manipulating people.

This handbook is based on many years of close study of the business of selling, plus a good deal of personal experience. I am the chairman of a magazine publishing company, which could not survive without good salesmen. As a publisher, I sell concepts and rely on their help to make them work. As an editor, I sell the ideas of a fine team of contributors. As a writer, I sell my own, but even that would not be possible without the efforts of the salesmen at Sidgwick and Jackson. My thanks to them all.

What Makes a Salesman Super?

Winners and Losers

If I had to name one characteristic which is absolutely essential to selling I would say *optimism*. It is hard to conceive of a supersalesman who is a pessimist. You simply *have* to believe that you are going to succeed, however many knocks you may have to cope with along the way. Selling is a job noted for its stresses and strains, and the person who loses heart easily is all too likely to have a nervous breakdown. He – or she – should choose a less demanding career.

Some people are born optimists. Others have to be taught. I'm not joking – there are schools on both sides of the Atlantic which do just that. 'Successful people,' says Dr David Schwartz, who has sold more than a million copies of *The Magic of Thinking Big*, 'are just ordinary folk who have developed belief in themselves and what they can do.' His advice: 'Eliminate the word "impossible" from your thinking. "Impossible" is a failure word. The thought "It's impossible" sets off a chain reaction of other thoughts to prove you're right.'

Paul J. Meyer, founder of the Success Motivation Institute in Texas, agrees. His courses are based on the principle that everyone is locked into the world of his own imagination. 'If you see yourself as a middle-income earner, and if you find it ludicrous to think of yourself as anything else, the odds stack up to near certitude that you will not in fact become anything else.' So the SMI tries to 'expand the narrow horizons that cramp men's lives'.

W. Clement Stone, who started as a door-to-door salesman and went on to build a fortune estimated at over $400 million, urges people to develop what he calls PMA – a Positive Mental Attitude. His formula is basically a type of auto-suggestion. You start your success course by telling yourself how marvellous you are. Have you ever considered, he asks, the battles you won before you were born? 'Just think, hundreds of thousands of sperm cells participated in a great battle yet only one of them won – and that one is *you*.'

The next step is to plant a number of 'self-motivators' – simple slogans – in your subconscious mind by repeating them every morning and night and at odd hours during the day. When these have taken root you no longer need to think about them, and in the midst of any business situation the correct self-motivator will assert itself and guide you automatically in the direction of success. The key phrase is *Do it now*! Whenever the signal *Do it now!* is flashed from your subconscious to your conscious mind, act immediately; with practice you will develop a reflex response so powerful that you will take action come what may.

Most people, says Stone, fail to develop all the useful self-motivators naturally as they grow to adulthood. Confronted with an opportunity that involves some element of risk, they tend to back off. They prevaricate. The opportunity evaporates before their eyes. Then they blame a capricious fate for their bad luck. This kind of experience, repeated over and over again, confirms them in the belief that they are born losers. The PMA technique changes all this. It gives them self-confidence and turns them into winners.

I used to make fun of Mr Stone's slogans – it's easy to do – but I have come to accept the merits of PMA. You *can* programme your mind. Muhammad Ali was an expert at this, and I have no doubt that it contributed to his impressive successes in the ring. His psyching-up process, before a fight, consisted of telling himself – and everyone else who would listen – 'I am the greatest.' It gave him confidence and helped to demoralize his opponents. It also, of course, sold a lot of tickets.

But optimism has to be realistic. You cannot afford to indulge in wishful thinking. Self-confidence is a great asset, but it must be based on a sound assessment of one's abilities and a thorough understanding of people, markets and the techniques employed in selling. Supersalesmen do not act on blind faith; they do their homework. Let us, therefore, take a closer look at some of the basic ingredients of success. They apply to every kind of business venture but are especially important if you want to be a supersalesman.

Fear of failure

One of the biggest obstacles to success is fear of rejection, fear of failure. Many people suffer from anticipatory dread, which has a paralysing effect. So much of selling involves putting one's ego on the line, and they are terrified of that awful word 'no'.

The obvious way to avoid failure is never to try at all. Don't pick up the telephone, don't call on people, don't make presentations, don't attempt to close a deal. But people with this kind of attitude shouldn't be in the business of selling. The supersalesman isn't afraid of rejection. He knows that it comes with the job. There is nothing personal about it: life is like that. You can't expect to be successful all the time. Even the best people have days when nothing seems to go right.

He also knows, however, that other opportunities await him. He learns from his setbacks, but he doesn't dwell on them. He doesn't allow past failures and defeats to dim his enthusiasm.

The supersalesman is a firm believer in having a go. He recognizes that you can't win a game without entering it. A man who shuns the gaming table is never going to win a fortune in Las Vegas. A man who hates the thought of getting involved in a business venture is never going to have the pleasure of seeing it grow and make millions. A salesman who is afraid of his customers is never going to win a lucrative contract.

It doesn't mean that one shouldn't worry. If you care about the things you are doing, you will naturally be anxious about the outcome. The important thing, though, is to learn to worry constructively. It means looking ahead at every step of the game to see what might go wrong – and working out what to do if it does.

One of the most telling differences between optimists and pessimists is the view they tend to take of change – change in technology, in the business climate, in the way things are done. The pessimist sees it all in doomsday terms; to him, it is a calamity. The optimist *welcomes* change because it provides new opportunities. He recognizes that every adversity has the seeds of equal, if not greater, benefit.

Take economic recessions. They make life harder for the businessman and force some companies into bankruptcy. But, as the late Paul Getty never tired of pointing out, they also force companies to become more efficient and they make it possible to pick up bargains. Getty recalled buying one of New York's top hotels at a knock-down price at a time when, as he put it, 'the gloom-and-doom chaps were too busy titillating their masochistic streaks with pessimistic predictions of worse times to come to recognize such bargains as this when they saw them'.

Getty once told me, at a party, that I would never get anywhere if I tried to be a conformist. I agreed whole-heartedly, saying that I had just read one of his books, *How to be Rich*, which made a strong case for boldness. Could I ask him a few questions? Yes, sure. Had it been easy? No; nothing ever was. Had there been moments of doubt? Silly boy, of course there had. What advice did he have for people who wanted to make it big? 'Ignore the pessimistic auguries of the self-appointed prophets of doom.'

Getty started his long career at the bottom – as a roustabout on an oil drilling site – and ended up as the richest man in the world. It's hard to argue with that kind of success.

Imagination

Paul Meyer was surely right when he talked about people being 'locked into the world of their own imagination'. Most of us are content to plod on in the same old way, regarding it as the natural order of things. The imaginative salesman not only welcomes change, but tries to be ahead of it. He is receptive to new ideas and is not afraid of innovation. He keeps a close watch on market trends and exploits the complacency of large corporations.

He also has the ability to look at products and services from the point of view of the customer. Many salesmen are chiefly concerned with themselves: their needs, their targets, their ambitions. The supersalesman recognizes the importance of learning to think like the prospect – he has the imagination to see things *his* way.

Enthusiasm

Salesmanship, someone once said, is nothing more than a 'transfer of enthusiasm'. It is a valid point. Enthusiasm is infectious: if you are genuinely excited about something there is a good chance that others will come to feel the same way.

Christopher Colombus – to give just one example – was enthusiastic about finding a western passage to the Indies. He painted such an exciting picture of wealth and prestige that the Spanish Court decided to give him the necessary ships, crews and funds. We all know the outcome: he discovered the New World.

The enthusiastic salesman has two other valuable attributes: abundant energy and a cheerful disposition. Like everyone else, he may occasionally feel angry, resentful, bitter, despondent. But the mood seldom lasts for long, and he generally takes care not to show it.

Concentration

Enthusiasm has to be focused: motivation comes from having a definite target to which you can direct your flow of energy. Many salesmen confuse activity with accomplishment. They rush from one useless appointment to another, determined to cram in more calls into the day than anyone else. Ask them to say what they have achieved and they look hurt. They have seen a dozen people. No, they haven't actually sold anything, but they have been *very* busy. More careful advance preparation, and a little more concentration on key prospects, would have produced far better results.

Stephen Leacock, the famous Canadian economist, once said about a friend that he 'jumped upon his horse and rode madly off in all directions'. The supersalesman may go from project to project, but he is selective and he tackles each one with single-minded determination.

Persistence

Every salesman hopes for a quick sale, so that he can move on to the next prospect. But there are times when your patience will be sorely tried: many people are slow to make up their minds and you may well be tempted to give up. The supersalesman never does. He knows the value of persistence, especially if big money is at stake.

Ray Kroc, the founder of McDonald's, was a great believer in persistence. He had a plaque on his office wall which spelled out his creed: 'Nothing in the world can take the place of persistence. Talent will not; nothing is more common than unsuccessful men with talent. Genius will not; unrewarded genius is almost a proverb. Education will not;

the world is full of educated derelicts. Persistence and determination alone are omnipotent.'

Sincerity

Many people take the same view of salesmen as they do of politicians: they *expect* them to lie, or at least to distort the truth. It is, of course, a very good reason why one shouldn't do it. The salesman who will say *anything* to get an order (they do, alas, exist) will soon find himself without prospects, without customers, and probably without a job. Ask Richard Nixon.

Genuine sincerity is an asset; phoney sincerity is a liability. The word itself has an interesting history. When Rome first acquired prosperity, its leaders decided to replace the public buildings, then mostly brick and wood, with grander edifices of stone or marble. Some of those who sold the marble weren't honest. They had their slaves rub wax into the cracks of marble slabs, blocks and pillars to make them look perfect. But when the weather beat upon the wax it washed away and the cracks reappeared. So the Senate passed a law: all marble sold for public buildings must be *sine cera* – without wax. Anyone selling waxed marble after that was severely punished. '*Sine cera*' later became 'sincere' in our language. Today's salesmen, too, should be without wax.

Almost as bad as telling lies is to break a promise. Some people are appallingly casual about this. They make promises even though they have serious doubts about their ability to deliver. If pressed, they make some feeble excuse. Word soon gets around that such people cannot be trusted. If you say that you are going to do something, *do it*. If you can't do it, or don't want to, don't say you will.

Memory

A good memory is immensely helpful; a bad memory can be a terrible handicap. Wives and girlfriends are understandably upset if you forget birthdays and anniversaries; customers get equally annoyed if you forget an appointment or change your story because you can't remember what you said the last time you met. Some salesmen forget pertinent facts, others dry up in the middle of a presentation because they can't remember what they are supposed to say next.

The supersalesman puts as much effort into developing a good memory as he does into everything else. He is particularly aware of the importance of remembering names. He knows that the simple act of remembering a name can put people on your side at once – and that, by the same token, forgetting a name, or getting it wrong, can wreck a deal.

Some people try to avoid this embarrassment by trying to trick a customer into giving his name before he realizes that it has been forgotten. The trouble is that it doesn't always work. You have probably heard the old story about the man who met a business acquaintance whose name he couldn't recall. He tried to pretend that he knew it but wasn't sure of the spelling, so he asked: 'How do you spell your name again?' The reply was: 'The only way it can be spelled, J.O.N.E.S.' Then there is the classic example of the salesman who always asked people whose names he had forgotten whether they spelled it with an *e* or an *i*. This was fine, until he tried it with Mrs Hill.

The main reason that most people forget a name is that they never remembered it in the first place. How often have you been introduced to someone new whose name you couldn't quite catch? You probably felt that you would never meet him or her again, so you said: 'Nice to meet you.' The supersalesman is more careful: if in doubt, he asks the person to repeat it. No one really minds if you do so – once. He then makes a point of using it wherever and whenever it seems to fit, which etches the name more firmly into his mind.

People have tried various methods of improving their

memory. Experts generally emphasize two basic points: observation and association. Observation means noting everything about a situation – or a person – and connecting two (or more) things to each other. Say 'Wall Street' and you think of bankers and stockbrokers. Say 'travel' and you think of planes or hotels. Say 'Arab' and you think of oil.

But this still leaves an awful lot of room for mistakes. A sensible precaution is to *write down* everything you have learned about a prospect as soon as you can – his name, the name of his company, his title, and anything which might be useful later on.

Most of us are better at remembering faces than names, so it may help to record the main features – his hair, his nose, his teeth. If he tells you about his work, his hobbies, or his family, make a note of that, too. He will be flattered, next time you meet him, that you have not only remembered his name but also his various interests. A good index card system can be a great ally.

HORSE TRADE

There is a lesson for every supersalesman in the story of the owner of a successful racehorse who, having resisted all temptation to sell it, is naturally dismayed when it dies.

He rings up a man who has frequently offered to buy the horse and asks if he is still interested. The man says yes, and sends along a cheque, which is cashed at once. The horse is put into a crate and sent to him. Astonishingly, there is not one word of protest.

Sometime afterwards the two men meet in the street. The buyer says he is happy with the deal: 'It was such a famous horse that I decided to raffle him at $25 a ticket. Thousands of people sent in money and I made a handsome profit.' But, says the former owner, what about the winner? How did he feel when he discovered that the horse was dead?

'Oh,' said the buyer cheerfully, '*I gave him his money back*.'

Listening

The popular image of the salesman is that of a glib talker –
someone with the 'gift of the gab'. The ability to communi-
cate is certainly useful – indeed, essential – but the supersalesman knows that much more can usually be gained by
listening.

A good listener not only makes a favourable impression
but also picks up a lot of valuable clues. Effective listening –
really hearing what the other person is saying – will tell you
a great deal about his desires, needs and anxieties. Bad
salesmen keep telling prospects what they think they
should have. Good salesmen allow them to say what they
want.

Making a Choice

Several other basic questions have to be tackled before one can hope to become a supersalesman. They may seem obvious, but a surprisingly large number of people never get around to giving them the serious consideration they so clearly deserve.

What do you want to sell?

Some people boast that they can sell *anything*, and they may well be right. But it is hard to become a supersalesman unless you genuinely believe in your product or service. Customers are quick to spot insincerity. How can you hope to persuade others to buy what you have to offer if your own attitude is one of indifference or, worse, cynicism?

If you are selling life insurance only in order to make a living you won't do nearly as well as the person who thinks that selling life insurance is the most important thing in the world. The same goes for just about everything else. It pays, therefore, to choose a field in which you have a keen interest and a product or service which you really believe in. Rejection is a lot easier to take if you have faith in what you are selling; the salesman who lacks that faith is bound to have a miserable time.

If you have already embarked on a career in sales, and you are unhappy about your product or service, don't hesitate to switch to something else. Selling should be fun. If you are about to embark on a sales career, ask yourself which of the many fields would suit you best. Computers? Drugs? Travel? Cars? Advertising? Financial services?

Then look for an employer who offers what you consider to be the best product or service in that field.

What kind of people do you want to sell to?

Some salesmen are good at selling to specialists; others get more pleasure out of dealing with the general public. Again, try to make an honest assessment. If you enjoy the company of specialists, this may be the ideal path for you. If you are a gregarious type who likes meeting people from all walks of life, you may be happier in a job which involves daily contact with ordinary customers. Do you like travelling? If so, look for a job which will give you the opportunity to do so. Don't settle for second best and then spend all your time complaining – as, alas, so many salesmen do.

What kind of company do you want to work for?

Some salesmen like working for large blue-chip organizations; others prefer the challenge offered by smaller companies. It is very much a matter of personal preference and judgment. Big companies have more clout and generally provide more security – though that can no longer be taken for granted in these uncertain times. But they also tend to be rather impersonal and the corporate hierarchical system makes it more difficult to act on your own initiative: every decision has to be referred to a superior and it is all too easy to get involved in tiresome office politics. There is usually a lot of boring paperwork and promotion can be discouragingly slow.

Small companies offer a wider range of duties and responsibilities, there is more scope for creative intuition and decision-making, and there is usually a better team spirit and a greater chance of promotion. Rewards are often superior to those available in large companies and you are more likely to gain the kind of experience which will enable you to reach the ultimate goal of many supersalesmen:

starting your own business. On the minus side, you will almost certainly have to work much harder and you will find it more difficult to hide failure. Small companies often jump from one crisis to another, and there is a high casualty rate.

A great deal, obviously, depends on your personality. Some people are natural organization men who would be totally lost in a small business; others are rugged individualists who would feel equally out of place in a large business.

We live in an era of transition: traditional industries are declining and new ones are taking their place. Changes in population – its size, age structure, composition, educational status and income – also have important consequences. They have a major impact on what will be bought, by whom and in what quantities. Many are predictable. We know, for example, that birth rates in developed countries will almost certainly continue to fall, that the service sector is likely to grow faster than manufacturing, and that life expectancy will go on rising – which, taken, together with a falling birth rate, means that the average age of the population will be higher than in the past.

These changes are significant for entrepreneurial salesmen and young people who are thinking about a career in sales. Here are some of the fields which are likely to show useful growth in the decades to come:

Retirement communities; Financial services; Health care; Information technology; Genetic engineering; Travel; Security services; Robotics; Cable television.

Managing Your Time

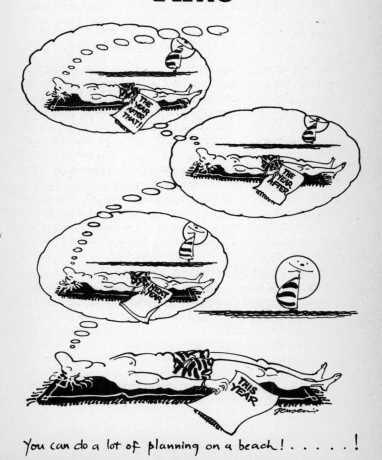

You can do a lot of planning on a beach! . . . . . !

Time Is Money

Many salesmen are good at selling but bad at managing their time. They are the harassed characters who rush around like mad and complain that there are not enough hours in the day. Time is one of life's great equalizers. Everyone – rich or poor, intelligent or stupid – has the same allotment of 24 hours a day, 365 days a year. But some people use it more effectively than others. They know that the key to good time management is to work smarter, not harder. In sales you are paid for results, not for your hours.

The problem for salesmen, of course, is that they are to some extent at the mercy of others. It is difficult to tell a customer to 'hurry it up'. They also tend to move around much more than people who have a fixed work location and schedule – and, as we all know, there is nothing much you can do about a traffic jam. Last, but not least, it's easier to allow yourself a diversion or delay because you don't have to punch a time clock.

Some of the techniques suggested in seminars on time management may, therefore, strike you as inappropriate. Only you can really judge whether you are making the best use of your time. A day spent with a wealthy prospect may well produce far better results than a day spent in the office making a dozen telephone calls. People are not machines, and no one expects you to act like one. But a time-conscious *attitude* can be of great help in producing the rewards you seek. And some of the basic rules of time management can be applied to just about every field, including sales. Here they are:

Elimination

Consider you past week's work and ask yourself, honestly, whether you have made the most effective use of your time. How much of that week was taken up with activities which, in retrospect, seem to have been quite unnecessary? If the answer is 'none', congratulations. But the chances are that some, at least, could have been eliminated without difficulty.

Meetings are the biggest time-wasters, especially in large organizations. They are usually held by people who have nothing better to do. How many did you attend last week, and how many were really important? How many are scheduled for this week, and how many could you give a miss?

Paperwork is another chore which most salesmen detest. A lot of it may seem essential, but did you really *have* to write that long-winded memo or report? Could you have made your point more quickly in person, or by phone? Did you have to write so many letters? How many could have been eliminated if you had simply picked up the telephone?

Organization

There are all kinds of aids which you can use in time management: diaries and time logs, a notebook with frequently used telephone numbers, desk computers, dictating machines, car telephones and so on. But the most effective method is, quite simply, to plan your day, week, or month.

The supersalesman sets himself goals and decides how he is most likely to get the hoped-for results. He makes it a firm habit, each evening, to write down all the things he must do tomorrow to make the most of that day, and numbers them in order of importance.

There will, inevitably, be times when you get sidetracked or when others make it impossible to meet a target.

But without definite goals, and a plan for reaching them, you have no clear sense of direction and are certain to waste a lot of your valuable time. You are just another hit-and-miss salesman.

In setting targets, try to be specific. Don't say, 'Increase sales in May.' Say, 'Increase sales by 20 per cent in May.' Work out the maximum, average and minimum results you can expect from each goal you set. This will help you to establish which are the most important.

Priorities

Getting one's priorities right is easier said than done. Some projects may have high priority because you say so, and some because someone else does. If your sales director or chief executive asks you to concentrate on a task, you can't very well tell him to jump into the nearest lake – tempting though it may be.

Even if you are in a position to set your own priorities, the answers are seldom clear cut. You have to decide that spending time on a project is more important than spending it in dozens of other possible ways. You may well make a bad judgment and not discover for some time afterwards

---

One aid you can well do without, when visiting prospects, is a digital timepiece which buzzes or emits a squeak when your allotted time for a certain task is up. It may be handy if you are chairing a meeting of your own staff, who can't protest, but customers are not going to be pleased with your meticulous precision. They feel they have the right to set the pace, and noisy reminders that you have other things to do are almost guaranteed to put them off. You can, of course, laugh and say something like: 'It's time to take my pill,' which is OK if you can instantly produce a box of pills. But it is far better to leave the wretched thing at home or in the office.

---

that you have backed the wrong horse. But it is clearly essential to have a strategy. The supersalesman charts all the projects he is involved with and looks at them objectively to determine which are the most vital. He tries to keep them in focus and doesn't waste time on calls which have low potential or on projects which have a relatively small chance of being successful.

Deadlines

Deadlines are a great help in overcoming indecision and procrastination. They have been part of my life ever since I first went into journalism thirty-five years ago and still play a key role in my own time management.

Some deadlines are imposed by others; some by myself. When I was writing a daily newspaper column, it was comparatively simple to meet them. Books and other projects which take months to complete are more difficult, but I know the value of assigning a definite time horizon to whatever I am doing. If a task has no deadline whatsoever, it is all too easy to put it off.

Again, it pays to take a look at your track record. If you do not meet deadlines well, ask yourself why. Are you being too optimistic, or is there some other reason? Some people miss deadlines because they have taken on too much, or because they have misjudged the time needed to complete a task. Some dislike finishing a project: they are perfectionists who like to hold on for more refinements or additions. Many do so because there is not enough pressure.

The method that works best for me is to decide how long something should take and use that date as a deadline, with a few extra days for safety. If I miss it, I analyse the factors which contributed to my failure and try to do better next time. If I get it right, I celebrate.

The biggest problem, though, is to decide what to do about other people's tardiness. A favourite trick of editors is to set a deadline which is well ahead of the date on which the material is actually needed. It often works for production managers, too. But what do you say to a *customer* who promises to let you have a decision by a certain date and then keeps you waiting for weeks, if not months, beyond it? Try to discover the reasons for the delay. He may simply be reluctant to make up his mind, in which case a little pressure won't do any harm. Or he may have temporary problems, in which case you simply have to be patient. But it is also possible that he no longer wants to do business with you but lacks the guts to say so. If you sense that this is the true reason, cut your losses and move on to the next project.

Holidays

Many salesmen insist that they have 'no time for holidays'. This is nonsense. If you plan your year properly, you should have time for at least a fortnight's break – most likely during a month like August, when business in many fields tends to be slack. Holidays are not a luxury but a necessity. They recharge your batteries and give you a chance to reflect. The supersalesman uses his holiday time to review his progress, to assess his various projects and to plan ahead. You can do a lot of useful thinking on a beach.

The Art of Delegation

The head of a large corporation once told me his basic approach to time management: 'Never do anything which you can get others to do for you.'

Some people find this hard to accept. Their motto goes to the other extreme: 'If you want something done right, you have to do it yourself.'

They hate to delegate because they have little faith in their subordinates and because they entertain fantasies of omnipotence or indispensability, imagining that they alone can carry out important tasks. It comes as an awful shock when they have a heart attack and find that they are not, after all, indispensable.

People who are afraid of delegation seldom rise to the top levels in management because of their apparent inability to train others and give them responsibility. They tend to get stuck at the level where they *can* do everything themselves.

Salesmen, I concede, do not always have access to people who could help them with their work. But even people with secretaries often insist on performing routine tasks like filing, making the coffee, photocopying and opening their mail. They waste a great deal of time which could be put to more productive use.

The supersalesman knows that delegation can buy more working time. It helps him to eliminate, pass on, or at least minimize routine jobs that keep him from his primary work. It frees him from trying to do everything and not doing anything as well as it should be done.

The first thing to do, obviously, is to determine what can

and should be delegated. Could someone else do that wretched paperwork? An independent salesman of my acquaintance, who has no secretary, uses a retired colleague to do a lot of it on a fee basis. He reckons that he earns more than enough extra money through the efficient use of time to make the arrangement worthwhile. Could an assistant take over some of your 'maintenance selling' so that you have more time to chase new business? Could he or she deal with prospects which have relatively low potential

TIME-WASTERS

Unplanned (and unnecessary) meetings
Office politics
Gossiping
Executive toys
Traffic jams
Illegible hand-written letters
Doing other people's jobs
Reading *Playboy*
No-shows
Making coffee
Long-winded memos

Drop-in visitors
Bureaucratic paperwork
Hunting for files
Telephone freaks
Re-drafting letters and reports
Interruptions
Arguing with secretaries
Talking to bookmakers
'Fire-fighting'
Procrastination
Personal calls

TIME-SAVERS

Checklists
Time logs
Speed-dial telephones
Answering machines
Desk computers
Action files
Targets
Deadlines
Confirmed appointments
Car telephones

Standardized letters
Daily 'to do' lists
Telephone amplifiers
Conference calls
Efficient secretaries
Speed-reading
Delegation
Qualifying prospects
Card systems
Dictating machines

so that you can concentrate on those which hold the promise of big pay-offs?

Giving people new and challenging things to do often produces surprisingly good results. (Which may be one reason why some salesmen refuse to delegate: they are afraid of competition from those who work for them.) If you don't show faith in their abilities, they will grow bored and indifferent. The best ones will look for another job.

There may, of course, be occasions when they make a mess of things and you have to do some 'fire-fighting'. You may even lose an account, though that shouldn't happen if you have kept an eye on them. But it is generally worth taking the risk.

I learned a long time ago that I could not possibly do my job as chairman of a magazine publishing company without careful delegation. I try to focus on the tasks I am good at – creating and selling new concepts, and editing. I leave all the rest to my able colleagues. I interfere only if there is a crisis.

This, I believe, is the right way to run a growing business. It is also the right way to become a supersalesman. You don't have to delegate *everything*: there are some jobs (especially the most difficult) which you must do yourself. But you have a far greater chance of success if you can find good people and allow them to show what they can do. Make sure that they understand what is expected of them, push them to do it, don't solve problems for them unless you really have to, and remember to praise good work.

Delegation multiplies results. If you do it all yourself, you can only get so much done. If you get others to help, you can achieve a great deal more.

Punctuality

'Punctuality is the politeness of kings' said – of all people – Louis XVIII, the last Bourbon King of France. It is, perhaps, as well that he never got around to visiting countries like Brazil or Egypt. He might have turned up on time, only to find that there wasn't one single flag, one single trumpeter, one single noble with a chain around his neck, one single member of a loyal crowd cheering himself hoarse. He would have been well advised to turn up two hours later – *that* would have been the proper politeness of a king.

Salesmen are, as a rule, punctual people because they don't want to be discourteous and because they are understandably anxious not to waste their own valuable time. They hate to be kept waiting and are furious if an airline makes them late for an important meeting. I am a very punctual person myself, partly because I spent some years presenting a BBC news programme, *The World at One*, which required strict time-keeping. I still tend to agree with one of Shakespeare's characters who said: 'Better to be three hours too soon than one minute too late.' But I have learned to accept that not everyone regards punctuality as a virtue.

Concern with being on time is an Anglo-Saxon tradition which puzzles a lot of other breeds: Spaniards, South Americans, Arabs. They tend to take the view that punctuality is one of the enemies of true freedom. If you want to do business with them, you have to slow down to their pace.

If in Rio de Janeiro you had scheduled an appointment for 10 a.m., and showed annoyance because your customer turned up at 11.30 a.m., you would be regarded as distinctly odd. He will give you a disarming smile and explain that he met a friend along the way who invited him for a cup of coffee and a chat. It would have been impolite to refuse. The explanation is given with such innocent charm that it would be churlish to point out that it was hardly polite to keep *you* waiting for so long.

People who expect instant action tend to be viewed with amusement, as I discovered on my own first visit some years ago. The BBC had sent me to make two television documentaries – one on inflation (then, as now, an horrendous problem) and the other on coffee. The Brazilians were charming and promised to give us every possible co-operation. But they refused to take our anxious talk of deadlines seriously. The sun was shining; it would be more

---

One often sees a number of clocks at airports or in hotels showing what time it is in various parts of the world. Here is my own guide, showing what '7 p.m.' means in different cities.

Stockholm: 7 p.m. precisely
Rome: Any time after 9 p.m.
Washington: 7.12 p.m.
Paris: 8 p.m.
London: 7.15 p.m.
Rio de Janeiro: Any time you feel like it. *Mañana* will do
Frankfurt: 7.02 p.m.
Madrid: No one would ever invite you to dinner at 7 p.m. – around 11 p.m. is nearer the time for an early evening meal, but no one will mind if you turn up at 11.30 p.m.
Sydney: 7.30 p.m.
Cairo: After 9 p.m.; around 10 p.m. is considered reasonable
Vienna: 7.20 p.m.
Jakarta: Indonesia operates on 'rubber time', which means anything between 8 p.m. and 11 p.m., or not at all

---

sensible, they said, to go on the beach. Meantime, all the necessary arrangements would be made. This went on day after day. Finally we settled for the obvious solution: we made our film about inflation on Copacabana beach and flew to Sao Paulo – where, mercifully, it was raining – for the one on coffee.

There really isn't much you can do about this sort of thing if you are chasing an order from a Latin or Middle East businessman. Don't set yourself a tight schedule, confirm appointments before you actually leave the hotel, and use your waiting time to study reports or make notes for your next meeting. If you find it hard to be patient, stick to doing business in Anglo-Saxon countries.

Dressing to Sell

Packaging your Appearance

The way you dress not only has an important bearing on the way you feel; it also influences the opinion others have of you. Appearance is generally a major factor in the judgments people make about a salesman. If he looks shabby it will naturally be assumed that he hasn't made a sale in months. If he neglects his appearance because he considers it to be unimportant, people will conclude that he is liable to be just as sloppy in his business dealings. The badly dressed salesman is invariably regarded as a loser.

The right clothes can do a lot for your ego and morale: if you look good, you will feel good. The wrong clothes can make you self-consciously defensive, and add to whatever sense of inadequacy you may have. Supersalesmen pay a lot of attention to their wardrobe: they do their best to look like people of substance and generally exude an air of assured, affluent elegance.

Walk into any expensive restaurant and study the people around you. Some will be totally at ease; they give the impression that they belong there. They dress to match the surroundings. Others will seem more like refugees from McDonald's who are there only because someone else is paying the bill. Which group inspires more confidence?

We all know, of course, that appearances *can* be deceptive. Financial con-men have always been smartly dressed, and an expensive suit is no guarantee of competence or even affluence. Many millionaires look like people who have bought their clothes in a cheap chain store. (They probably have.) The rich are often careless about dress because they can't be bothered to make the effort and because they reckon, not without reason, that they can do as they please. The fact remains, nevertheless, that most of us base our judgments of others in large part on what they wear. The supersalesman knows that he cannot afford to let people think that he is sloppy and/or unsuccessful.

Good clothes are one of the most worthwhile investments you can make. They will help you to project a positive image, and they tend to last longer than the cheaper kind. Poor fabrics lose shape and develop a tired, bedraggled look. The cost may seem daunting at first, but you will find that it pays off handsomely. So buy the best, even if it means borrowing from the bank or taking out a second mortgage.

Dress like those with whom you wish to be associated. If you don't want to be mistaken for a door-to-door salesman, don't dress like one. Aim to look upper middle class. This makes decision-makers feel that you are one of them, and makes it easier to deal with underlings who stand in the way. If you want to command respect from secretaries and clerks, you must dress like the people in their lives who represent authority to them.

In the business world, this traditionally means conservative, well-tailored 'classic' suits in blue or grey, made from wool or wool blends. The medium-to-dark grey is a likeable yet serious colour, but the general rule is: 'The more serious the selling situation, the more serious the colour of the suit.' But there are times and places which call for a different approach. If you are selling to farmers, for example, a tweed jacket would probably be more appropriate. Californians are fond of leisure suits and Texans may be more accommodating if you demonstrate your regard for the Lone Star State by wearing cowboy boots. In the tropics, safari suits are popular and in the Philippines the *barong tagalog*, a frilly native shirt, is accepted as formal evening wear in place of a tuxedo.

But don't overdo it. Adapting yourself to local surroundings

carries its own pitfalls. An English banker would probably feel ridiculous in cowboy boots, and it would almost
certainly show. A Wall Street stockbroker would look
equally absurd in flowing Arab robes and headgear. You
should never risk a possible accusation that you are mock-
ing other people's customs.

Here are some basic guidelines, based on conversations
with successful salesmen:

Suit your shape

Your clothes should compliment you, the individual, not
distract or highlight problem areas. Large salesmen often
frighten customers with their imposing presence, and it
may pay to tone it down by wearing light suits in grey or
beige. A white shirt is probably best; with it, wear a bright,
cheerful tie. Small men, who need to increase their authority, should wear dark suits (pinstripes are fine), white shirts,
heavy glasses (if they need them) and silk ties. Stocky men
should wear smooth, thin materials, not heavy, tweedy
fabrics.

Whatever your shape, avoid those awful suits with broad
stripes. Salesmen have quite enough to cope with already:
don't lumber yourself with the extra liability of looking like
an offspring of Al Capone.

Beware of high fashion

It is tempting to adopt the latest fashion, but unless you are
actually involved in selling it you would be well advised to
resist the urge to become a trend-setter. It may work for
journalists, advertising executives and novelists (who are
all expected to be a little eccentric) but salesmen who look
like they have just stepped out of the pages of a men's
fashion magazine run the risk of not being taken seriously.
This is particularly true of the financial world, but it also
applies to many other fields. Large corporations, who tend
to have fairly strong ideas about corporate dress, prefer to

deal with people who look like their own executives. Stay clear of shiny suits, fancy buttons, strange-coloured stitching and flamboyant colours.

Get a good fit

Many salesmen buy clothes which don't really fit them because they hate to admit that they have put on weight. They tell themselves that the suit, or shirt, will be 'all right as soon as I go on a diet'. Somehow, though, they never get around to it. So their jackets can't be buttoned up, their shirts and collars are too tight, and their trousers fight a losing battle with ever-growing waistlines. The effect is to make them look like slobs – and who wants to buy from a slob? Never pretend to yourself that you haven't changed when it is plain to everyone else that you have. Either start that diet or buy clothes that will comfortably accommodate your figure.

Pick the right tie

Ties say a lot about a man – his tastes, attitudes and social status. They are one of the first things other people – especially other men – notice when they first meet and should be chosen with great care. By all means try to express individuality, but never wear a tie that *shouts*. Large symbols, pictures and humorous messages should be avoided. Bow ties are widely reckoned to indicate a frivolous nature. Company ties are all right providing they are stylish – which, alas, all too many are not.

People at the top prefer to wear ties which indicate an élitist background: the right school, club, regiment, or professional group. If they don't qualify on any of these counts, they generally choose ties which are very similar. Polka-dots also look good with solid suits and shirts. Silk is easily the best material for ties, and there should be enough of it – ties that are too short look ridiculous. Make sure they reach your belt buckle.

Buy smart accessories

Accessories are as important as the clothes you wear and should be chosen with equal care. Extrovert salesmen have an unfortunate penchant for novel and flashy items, which no doubt contributes to the widespread feeling that they are not serious and, therefore, cannot be trusted. Leave those fancy belt buckles and chunky diamond rings to scrap metal dealers and people who sell used cars. The super-salesman prefers accessories which are simple and elegant. A thin, plain gold watch makes a far better impression than the latest gimmick.

Attaché cases should only be used to hold notes for presentations, contract forms, a discreet pocket diary and other essentials. Bring it along to a meeting, but *not* to lunch with a senior executive: he expects you to have all the salient facts in your head and won't be pleased if you rummage around your case just as you are settling down to the port or brandy. (Gentlemen's clubs take a particularly dim view of this kind of activity.) Pens should also look stylish; *never* ask anyone to sign a contract with one of those cheap half-chewed ball-point pens. Umbrellas should be black, with a plain handle. Business cards should be of modest size, with elegant lettering. *Never* print your company's sales message on a card: people who are that crass are aliens in the world of supersalesmen.

Get stylish sportswear

A lot of business is done – or at least initiated – during leisure activities and the judgments made about your appearance then matter as much as those made during office hours. So it makes sense to apply the same principle to sportswear: aim to look upper middle class, especially if you are asked to play golf or tennis (or go sailing) with the kind of people who are in a position to make big decisions.

Buy the kind of clothes you feel most comfortable in, and which you think will suit your personality, but make sure that they are of high quality and fit in with your surroundings. Don't turn up on a golf course (as, alas, some salesmen have been known to do) looking like an over-decorated Christmas tree, or on a sailing boat dressed like the captain of the *QE2*. You can't afford to have people laugh at you. Americans generally like brighter colours than Europeans (especially in areas like Florida and California) but garish combinations invariably produce negative reactions. The safest course is to stick to white, navy blue, khaki, or beige.

Play safe on formal occasions

Formal occasions provided earlier generations with a splendid excuse to dress up: European courtiers strutted about like peacocks. The clothes worn today are, by comparison, awfully dull. It is tempting to break with convention and some people do just that: they turn up wearing bright red frilly shirts, gaudy bow ties and tuxedos with fancy

LOOKING RIGHT

Good

Silk ties
Expensive cotton shirts
Small gold cuff-links
Grey and dark blue suits
Beige raincoats
Cashmere overcoats
Old school ties (if they are
    the right school)
Club ties (providing they
    are stylish)
Simple, small monograms
    on shirts
Brown leather attaché case
Smart, well-made shoes,
    preferably black
Pinstripe shirts
Thin, plain gold watch
Ribbon of the *Légion
    d'Honneur*
Dark blazers
Well-tailored safari suit
    (in tropics)
Neat hair; not necessarily
    short, but not too long
Horn-rimmed glasses
Handkerchief in breast
    pocket
Tweed jacket (when selling
    to farmers)

Bad

Green jackets
Short-sleeved shirts
Tight clothes
Multi-coloured shoes
Black raincoats
Shiny hair
Coloured handkerchiefs
Dark glasses
Leather jackets
Ostentatious monograms
Fancy belt buckles
Suits with broad stripes
Socks that show leg when
    you sit down
Beards (especially goatees)
Bow ties
See-through shirts
Pencil line moustache
Bowler hats
Fancy buttons
Tie pins or clasps
Solid red shirts
Suspenders
Big, flashy cuff-links
Cheap ball-point pens
Plastic briefcase
Dandruff

stitching. You may be able to risk it if your dining compan-
ions are all colleagues of roughly equal status, but if the
chairman of the Board (or chief executive) is present he
may take a dim view of such an ostentatious display of
individuality. If you are invited to a formal banquet given by
strangers it may reflect badly on your company. So it is
generally advisable to stick to the traditional black tuxedo –
or, when required, the even more formal white tie and tails.
But there is *some* scope for self-expression. White dinner
jackets are acceptable during the warm summer months
and will show that you are affluent enough to own more than
one type of evening dress. Frilly white cotton or silk shirts
also look good, and there is no reason why you should not
wear a dark blue or wine red bow tie instead of the
conventional black. Cummerbunds are OK providing you
are slim. Studs and cuff-links should be small, simple and as
expensive as you can afford.

Grooming

Some men think grooming isn't manly and, indeed, there are people who look effeminate because they obviously try *too hard*. You don't want customers to wonder how you have time for anything other than taking care of your hair, or to jump to the wrong conclusions because you smell like Joan Collins. But a certain amount of grooming is clearly an essential part of packaging your appearance. The trick is to make it all seem quite natural.

Hair

Don't let your barber talk you into experimenting with fancy hair styles: find a style that suits your face and personality and stick to it. Don't wear a hair piece or wig which is unnatural or exaggerated and attracts attention to itself, or comb your hair differently to cover a bald spot: people will look at your hair to see what you are trying to hide.

Yul Brynner and Telly Savalas turned baldness into an asset. You may find it hard to do the same, but desperate efforts to disguise what you (but not necessarily everyone else) regard as a defect will almost certainly attract ridicule.

A moderate length of hair is easily the best bet. It suggests pragmatic, serious, business-like qualities. A salesman with long, shaggy hair does not inspire confidence. Nor does a scraggly, unkept or exaggerated beard. Business leaders do not, on the whole, care for beards and I strongly recommend that you resist the urge to grow one. If you feel that you must wear a beard, make sure that it is neatly trimmed and of moderate length. The same goes for a moustache. A natural, well-trimmed moustache looks good on some men, but at all cost avoid the pencil thin or waxed-end moustache because it makes you look like a caricature.

Hair should be washed frequently (you can't afford

YOUR CAR

The perfect car for a supersalesman is, of course, the Rolls-Royce. It shows millionaires that you are one of *them*, which always makes it easier to do business with their kind, and persuades the rest of the world that you are a success.

Corporations, alas, tend to be reluctant to provide their star performers with such an obvious status symbol. This is partly because of the cost but the main reason is that the chairman doesn't want to be upstaged by one of his employees. You are free to buy your own, if you can afford it, but if you have your eye on a seat in the Boardroom it is advisable not to upset him with such an open gesture of defiance.

You are safer if your sphere of operations is well away from head office. Commander Whitehead, the supersalesman who put Schweppes on the map in America, used to drive a splendid white Rolls Royce through the streets of New York. His excuse: it was an advertisement for Britain.

At home, senior executives generally settle for a Rover or a Jaguar. Some would prefer a foreign car, such as a Mercedes or a BMW, but many corporations have a strict 'buy British' policy. Smaller companies are more amenable. They may even let you buy a Porsche. Sports cars impress other salesmen, and are permissible if you are selling advertising space or work in public relations. But there are many other fields (such as finance) where they are liable to say the wrong things about you.

Whatever you buy, make sure that your car has a telephone. It is not only very useful but conveys the impression that you are enthusiastic about your work.

dandruff) and cut every two or three weeks. By all means use colouring (blending some grey in a man's hair gives him character and the appearance of maturity) but stay clear of strong colours: jet-black hair, for example, tends to make your face chalky white. Sideburns should not extend past the centre of the ear. Use a gel to keep your hair neat, but avoid looking slick. Comb it just before a meeting, but *never* in front of anyone who matters.

Smell

Some women like the smell of essential man – 'the sweaty Tarzan bit' as one young lady once described it to me. But many more find it repulsive. So do most heterosexual businessmen. If you turn up smelling like a boxer after a heavy workout – or a seventeenth-century courtier – it doesn't really matter whether you are a champion or not. Your customers will be anxious to keep their distance and they won't be able to concentrate on what you are *saying*. Personal hygiene is of fundamental importance and there really is no excuse for neglecting it. A bath or shower every morning, with a generous application of soap, isn't a luxury but a *necessity*. Deodorants and colognes will keep you in good odour throughout the day. Don't overdo it – you don't want people to get the wrong idea – but make sure that you always smell clean and pleasant, especially on hot summer days.

Teeth

Salesmen are expected to do a lot of smiling, so nice teeth are a major asset. Few things are more off-putting than an ugly mouth with stained, crooked teeth and obvious gaps. It is often accompanied by bad breath, which can kill sales as well as romances.

The good news is that advances in dentistry have made it easier (and less painful) to do something about it. Modern drills revolve 450,000 times as fast as those used 30 years ago and are therefore less likely to jar the nerves. Anaesthetics are longer lasting and more precise. Dentists have also developed a variety of cosmetic procedures that include bleaching, which offers a temporary lightening of tooth stains, and the application of veneers – thin porcelain or acrylic façades that have been likened to false fingernails. By far the most popular technique is bonding, in which plastic resins are applied directly to the surface of teeth to mask chips, discolorations and cracks, or even to conceal unattractive gaps. It costs anywhere from one-third to one-half of the price of crowns and caps and can usually be performed without pain or the need to file down teeth.

Even if you are blessed with a good set of teeth, dental care is essential. See your dentist regularly, even if it is only to remove plaque, and use mouthwash to start every day.

The Name Game

Much time and effort is devoted to finding the right name for a product, yet most of us are surprisingly casual about our own names.

Names play a significant role in the way we perceive ourselves, the way others see us, and the way the two combine to influence attitudes and actions. If you are born a Rothschild or a Rockefeller you have a head start in the business world, even though a famous name doesn't guarantee competence. A Smith or Jones has to work much harder to reach the top. So if you think your name may be a handicap, consider changing it.

In showbiz they do it all the time. Hollywood felt, rightly, that the public wouldn't buy a star called Issur Danielovitch, so he became Kirk Douglas. Michael Caine started out as Maurice Micklewhite, Tony Curtis as Bernie Schwartz and Judy Garland as Frances Gumm. Charles Aznavour, believe it or not, used to be Varenagh Aznavourian and Maria Callas signed the hotel register as Maria Kalogeropoulou.

I made a mistake, at the age of fifteen, in taking my stepfather's prosaic name, Davis. Had I known that I would spend the rest of my life as a writer and broadcaster, I would have tried to be more imaginative. An author has a better chance of selling books if he has an unusual name, like Gore Vidal or Truman Capote. I really *ought* to do something about it.

The trouble with commonplace names is that they make no impact: you are regarded as just one of the crowd, which is quite the wrong image for a supersalesman. But, as

Let's see now...
John **A**bbe
or John **A**bberkerk
or John **A**bbensetts
or John **A**bbercorn
or John **A**.......

PHONE BOOK
A-D

A-D

PHONE BOOK E-K

K/M

N/R

Hollywood recognized, names which are hard to pro-
nounce can also be a liability.

Some people solve the problem by adopting new first or
middle names. If you are called Smith, there is much to be
said for making it Truman Smith or John Livingstone Smith.
Another useful ploy is to add a second surname and use a

hyphen, as in John Truman-Smith. 'I love hyphens,' said Katharine Hepburn in *Love Among the Ruins*, 'they inspire confidence.' So they do; goodness knows why.

A title, of course, is better still. We are all snobs, even if we like to pretend that we are not, and I don't think anyone would dispute that 'Sir John Smith' is superior to plain John Smith or, for that matter, Maurice Micklewhite. If for some inexplicable reason, the Queen hasn't yet got around to tapping you on the shoulder with her jewelled sword, or if you live in a country where they have foolishly abandoned titles, you can always invent one. There is no law against changing your first name to Duke or Prince.

Women have another option; they can marry a man with a title, or with an attractive name, and make it their own. Ardent feminists may disapprove, but ambitious women need all the help they can get.

'Bubbles'

Financial Games

The Paper Game

The financial world offers tremendous scope for the super-salesman. A skilful operator can make more money in a *day* than others do in a lifetime of selling cars or home computers.

Basically, the game involves turning paper into cash. The first great stock market speculation, early in the eighteenth century, centred around the South Sea Company, which had been granted a British Government franchise to exploit South America and the Pacific. The company had no assets other than the franchise, but its first public issue met with an enthusiastic response. Nobody was quite sure how much he stood to gain, but everyone felt certain that he would make a fortune. Other companies were hastily formed to cash in on the general mood of optimism. Many had bizarre objectives such as 'importing a large number of jackasses from Spain' and 'fishing wrecks from the Irish Coast'. One promoter announced, simply, that he was forming a company 'for an undertaking which shall in due time be revealed'. The bubble burst when the South Sea Company suddenly collapsed.

History repeated itself in the Wall Street boom of the 1920s. Encouraged by high-pressure salesmanship and daily reports of rising prices, all kinds of people (including taxi drivers and office boys) put their savings into stocks without bothering to find out what the companies actually did, or how well they did it. Caution was thrown to the winds. When the crash came in 1929, hundreds of thousands of gullible speculators were left penniless.

In the 1980s, the game is more likely to involve companies which are concerned with some aspect of modern technology. Many are new ventures which exist mostly on paper or which have only just got underway. The salesmen who issue the prospectus usually make a point of stressing the risks involved. They use phrases like 'there is absolutely no assurance that the company will ever make a profit' and 'the directors are in no position to pay dividends and may never be able to do so'. It may seem an odd method of selling, but it works. There are always people who are eager to 'get in on the ground floor' of what may just turn out to be a highly successful business.

To be fair, not all financial deals are based on such flimsy material. Many of the companies whose shares are offered to the public have a good track record; some are among the best-known names in industry. But, despite all the new regulations, there are still numerous enterprises which bear a close resemblance to the South Sea Company. And all offers involve some form of salesmanship.

Middlemen like bankers and stockbrokers raise funds for blue-chip companies by selling shares or some other type of paper to investors, including pension funds, insurance companies and other institutions. And they help entrepreneurs to turn their assets into cash by showing them how to 'go public'. The commissions they earn are often very substantial: they can add up to millions.

Not surprisingly, the big names of the financial world like to keep the main action to themselves. The outsider lacks the clout to compete with them. But even comparatively small firms manage to do quite well. Many concentrate on the more adventurous end of the business – the Unlisted Securities Market or the Over-the-Counter market.

The institutions are nowadays the largest buyers of stock, so much of the effort is focused on them. Sometimes, a telephone call is enough. But banks and stockbrokers frequently get their research departments to prepare elaborate and impressive presentations on the companies whose paper they want to sell, and, if necessary, they will arrange meetings with the directors and visits to the factory. They also have lists of affluent clients who may be interested in a new offer.

The game continues when the shares are sold, because there are always people who want to take their profit (or cut a loss) and others who think they are a good investment. So the sales force is permanently on the go.

But the supersalesman doesn't wait to be asked to do a deal. He creates 'buying opportunities'. Much of his day is spent calling prospects who may have some spare cash, or who can be persuaded to switch from one investment to another. Each transaction earns a commission, so a top salesman can make quite a lot of money without ever leaving his office. He doesn't have to be an investment expert himself: what counts is the ability to spin a plausible tale. The backroom boys of his firm will provide him with statistics and other useful information which he can use in his sales pitch.

On Wall Street, where they use much more aggressive selling techniques than they do in London or Paris, some salespeople try to strengthen their case by using absurd but attention-grabbing gimmicks. They claim to be able to tell what will happen to the market by studying sunspots, analysing dreams and using mass telepathy. Some even base confident forecasts on the ups and downs of hemlines.

I once met a stockbroker who insisted that stock prices share something with the mouse population of a twenty-acre field in central New York State. Both, he said, were governed by cycles. I was too stunned to ask him how he kept count, but I suppose his theory is no more idiotic than the one advanced by New York investment adviser Frederick Goldsmith, who said his information came from a daily newspaper comic strip. Each strip, he maintained, contained a market code. If, for example, the main character's right hand was in his pocket, the hidden signal meant 'buy'. If two puffs of smoke rose from his cigar, it meant that the second hour of trading would be especially strong.

Do people still fall for this kind of rubbish, 250 years after the South Sea fiasco? Sadly, some do. They will believe anything provided it is stated with enough conviction.

Even those of us who laugh at people like Goldsmith tend to be impressed by what we are led to believe is inside information. Salesmen often claim to be 'in the know', but it generally turns out to be mere guesswork dressed up as fact. The people most likely to have *genuine* inside information are company directors – and they are committing a crime if they divulge it or use it for their own benefit.

The buying and selling of paper has become a vast international business, partly because of modern communications but also because of the natural desire of most investors to spread their risks. The supersalesman does not acknowledge borders. It is not uncommon, these days, for teams of executives to arrive in other countries with briefcases full of graphs and statistics, determined to sell their wares. Japanese firms like Nomura Securities have become particularly aggressive, much to the annoyance of big American operators like Merrill Lynch, which for years has rejoiced in the appropriate nickname of 'The Thundering Herd'. Nomura frequently sends its salesmen on 'missions' to North America, visiting twenty or thirty institutions in a week. They carry detailed information to convince fund managers that no one in his right mind could refuse Japanese shares coupled with the firm's knowledge of the Tokyo stock market. The Nomura house magazine, published in English for the overseas branches, emphasizes teamwork, energy and the family atmosphere: its slogan is 'Together around the world'. The company also uses unorthodox methods at home: it has, for example, some 1,800 'salesladies', working on two-year contracts, who sell stocks on the doorstep in Japanese suburbs, mostly to housewives with savings from family income.

But the Japanese do not have it all their own way. European and American salesmen also go to Tokyo and Osaka to persuade the thrifty Japanese to invest in their enterprises. And they compete vigorously for the profitable business available from the Arabs and their Swiss (or British) advisers. They don't like to be called salesmen – the British are particularly snooty about this – so their business cards carry more fancy labels like 'investment bankers'. But selling is what they do, and the best of them do it remarkably well.

In Britain the Thatcher Government has done its best to promote wider share ownership, notably through the privatization of state-owned industries, because it sees obvious advantages in turning more and more people into capitalists: they have a vested interest in keeping the Tory party in power. Attempts to set up 'share shops' on the factory floor have been a flop, but some department stores have opened similar shops and there may well be others. The growing use of electronic gadgetry is also creating new sales opportunities. People can tap into information which was previously known to a privileged few, and in the years ahead they will be able to buy and sell shares from the home or office through their personal computers. Instant access to the market has already led to the creation of many new financial products.

But the field which still holds the greatest appeal for many salesmen is insurance – or, more specifically, life insurance. Much of it is sold through insurance brokers, who have direct contact with customers, and the big life companies go out of their way to provide every kind of back-up, including professional expertise. They also pay handsome commissions. It takes very little capital to set yourself up as an insurance broker and the man – or woman – who has a genuine flair for this branch of salesmanship can earn a great deal of money.

The Marriage Brokers

Mergers and acquisitions can provide handsome rewards for supersalesmen who specialize in arranging corporate marriages. They not only collect generous fees but also stand a good chance of making substantial capital gains.

Many such marriages are initiated by outsiders rather than by the managements of the companies involved. They spot an opportunity, put together a case, sell the idea to one or other of the potential partners and act as go-between. The job demands flair, an understanding of people and balance sheets, and an excellent range of contacts. Bankers and stockbrokers are ideally placed to act as matchmakers, which is why they get the bulk of the business, but there is also quite a number of lone operators who are content with a sizeable 'finder's fee'.

The simple operation

The most common type of deal involves the acquisition of a small company by a larger one. The marriage broker hears that someone is willing to sell his business, so he offers to help in return for a percentage of the eventual purchase price. He then goes to one of the bigger companies in the same field and shows why the deal makes good sense. He may have to talk to three or four prospective buyers and it may take months to bring the negotiations to a successful conclusion. But a good salesman usually has several possible deals going at the same time.

If the intended bride is a public company, there is nothing to stop him buying a parcel of shares *before* he embarks on his quest. This almost certainly guarantees him a nice profit if the deal succeeds, and gives him an extra incentive to sell the idea.

The friendly merger

The friendly merger may involve two companies which are in the same line of business and are roughly of equal size. The marriage broker persuades them that they would benefit by joining forces – that two and two make five. He arranges a straightforward share exchange and may well collect a fee from both.

The contested bid

Contested take-over bids are more tricky. The middleman goes to see the chief executive of a company which is known to be in a hurry to expand and draws his attention to a business which would fit very nicely into the existing set-up. He warns that the directors may put up a fight, but points out that they do not have a controlling interest and that a sufficiently generous bid is likely to be accepted by a majority of shareholders, despite the objections of the Board.

Contested bids may fail, which is why it is advisable to ask for your fee in advance. But they do have two obvious merits. If you have bought shares before going to see the chief executive, and the deal succeeds, you will almost certainly make much more money than you would have done if the merger had been friendly. Meanwhile, a lengthy battle is likely to produce sizeable fees for everyone involved in an advisory capacity.

The successful failure

A popular ploy in the 1980s is to arrange a bid which is bound to be rejected, but which allows the bidder to walk away with a huge profit. Some entrepreneurs (Rupert Murdoch is a prominent example) have made vast fortunes through successful failures. You accumulate a large share-holding, make a public bid and force the panic-stricken directors to mount a vigorous defence – which invariably puts up the price of the shares and hence the value of the holding. You then withdraw the offer and sell your shares. If you are lucky, the directors and their friends may even arrange to buy the shares from you at the higher figure, just to be rid of an unwelcome suitor. The supersalesman benefits in two ways. He gets a fee for spotting a suitable 'victim'. And he goes along for the ride by buying some shares himself at an early stage.

The self-financing bid

A clever operator can often buy another business *with its own money*. This is how Nigel Broackes started Trafalgar House, now one of Britain's largest companies. Broackes discovered that Commercial Union Assurance owned a company called Westminster and Kensington Freeholds, which it seemed to regard as something of a nuisance. Broackes, then twenty-seven, thought it had considerable potential and asked if it was for sale. Commercial Union said it was, but that it would prefer to invite tenders from several other parties to see what price it could get. Broackes offered £3,345,000, a sum which everyone knew he hadn't got, and was accepted. He raised the money by persuading the sellers to put up almost 100 per cent of the purchase price. The deal was his own idea, but if a marriage broker had drawn his attention to the company, and to the likely response of its owners, he would certainly have listened.

Funny money

The beauty of the merger game is that you don't necessarily need cash to finance a deal. If you are a publicly quoted company, paper will do just as well. The recipient can always sell it on the market. 'Funny money' is high-multiple stock (or, more simply, stock which sells more on faith than actual earnings) used by people in a hurry to buy other companies or raise capital. If often goes by curious names, such as '6 per cent cumulative redeemable partially convertible preference shares with options'.

How to join the action

This, obviously, is a field for specialists, but you don't *have* to be a financial genius to join in. A talent for salesmanship is more important.

The most sensible course is to take a job with one of the established firms and learn as much as you can. You will not only become thoroughly familiar with the tricks of the trade but will also make a lot of useful contacts. You are then in a good position to set up a business of your own. Try to find

---

One of the oldest games in the financial world is to sell something you haven't got.

The players are known as 'bears' and are among the more daring animals in the Stock Exchange menagerie. A bear sells stock he doesn't own in the hope that he can buy them at a lower price before delivery is due.

A concerted attack by speculators is known as a 'bear raid'. In a raid, a dozen or more people may *all* be selling shares they haven't got. The idea, of course, is to create a panic so that the price will drop. They then move in, buy at the lower level, deliver and pocket the difference.

It sounds like a splendid ploy, infinitely more attractive than selling baked beans or Volkswagens, but there is one obvious snag. You may be unable to buy the shares you need – or they may cost you a great deal more than you have bargained for. Another smart lot of operators, aware that you have gone out on a limb, may mount a 'bear squeeze'. Stock is withheld, so that prices have nowhere to go but up. A bear squeeze can be extremely painful.

---

partners who have skills which you lack: a good investment analyst, for example, will help to steer you in the right direction.

Prospects are not hard to come by. Hundreds of businesses are up for sale at any given moment. They may have fallen on hard times, or the chairman may have decided to pull out. Tax liabilities may compel important shareholders to sell, or the bank manager may be getting impatient. Sometimes a family quarrel opens the door to a lucrative deal. If the business is any good at all, there is bound to be someone who is interested in buying it. Many companies would rather grow through acquisitions than through the laborious process of creating and developing ventures of their own. Your job is to spot openings which others have missed and to sell your concepts to the people who are most likely to benefit.

Bright Ideas

From Fads to Riches

Any competent salesman can sell cars or airline tickets. The test of a supersalesman is whether he can sell something which people don't *need*.

Fortunes are regularly made by clever entrepreneurs who think up some fad and persuade millions to buy the stuff at fancy prices. The basic strategy is to find a product which will capture the imagination of the buying public and to make a killing before others get in on the act. Pet rocks, water beds, clone kits, rubic cubes and square eggs are all examples.

The simplest ideas often do best. When the 'flower power' cult got underway in California during the late 1960s, a Los Angeles couple driving down a freeway were intrigued to see several other cars which had been decorated with wild, bright colours. As they talked about the motivation behind this unusual touch, a thought came to the husband: perhaps the world was ready for some kind of bright, good-looking, easy-to-use, fun bit of madness to stick on cars and things. They went home, produced some stick-on flowers and covered their own car with them. Their neighbours laughed, but within a few days children started to come to their door asking if they could buy some flowers too.

A week later the couple had made their first sale to a store and orders were coming in from others. During the months that followed the fad not only caught on all over America but also found its way to such diverse places as Sweden, Japan, Germany, Mexico and Canada. The crazy little vinyl flowers even turned up on taxis in Cairo and phone books in Tel Aviv. By the end of the following year some 180 million had been sold for more than $10 million at retail.

The 'pet rock' was another successful gimmick. The very notion that a painted pebble could be sold for $4.95 struck me as utterly absurd when I first heard about it. I should have known better. On a *Punch* outing to Margate, a few months earlier, Jonathan Routh (of *Candid Camera* fame) had proved to me that you can sell just about *anything* if you can keep a straight face. He picked up a large pebble on the beach, wrote 'a present from Margate' on it, and offered it for sale to passers-by. I overheard the following conversation:

MUG: Well, it's very nice. But what can I do with it?

ROUTH: My dear fellow, it'll look *lovely* at the bottom of a goldfish bowl.

MUG: Yes, you're right. But I haven't got a goldfish bowl.

ROUTH: It's only ten pence. I ask you – what can you get for ten pence these days?

MUG: True. I'll take it.

If I hadn't been quite so busy falling about with laughter I, too, might have made a fortune. The man who marketed boxes of pet rocks in America, Gary Dahl, took $10,000 a *day*.

I don't know what Jonathan is doing right now, but it wouldn't surprise me to hear that he has gone into the antiques business. You need the same sort of cheek to explain the merits of wig stands, Victorian chimneypots, rusty keys and other useless rubbish to gullible tourists.

'A great key, sir. Used by Henry VIII himself, they say.'

'Yes, it's very nice. But what can I *do* with it?'

'Well, sir, you could get a lock made to fit it. Or it would make a lovely paperweight. Or you can leave it lying around on your office desk; keys are irresistible things to handle, and you can always tell people that it's the key to your wine cellar. Or you can use it as a key ring – see what I mean? Me, I'd start a collection. Now I happen to have this other key, used by Bonnie Prince Charlie, they say . . .'

Auction houses manage to unload the most unlikely items. At a sale in London, an American collector paid thousands of dollars for a man-hole cover, and another buyer acquired a mink G-string worn by the late Gypsy Rose Lee for $500. More bizarre still was the sale of a ten-foot propeller from a German first world war bomber.

The rich can clearly be persuaded to indulge in all kinds of foolishness. Neiman-Marcus, the famous Texas store, has long made a habit of producing Christmas catalogues designed to dazzle oil millionaires. They have offered things like midget submarines, gold omelette pans and life-size portable replicas of customers or their loved ones 'programmed to laugh as long as you like at your jokes and say "yes" in any language you choose at the touch of a remote control button'. But, as we have seen, the foolishness is not confined to those who have more money than sense. Fads have a broad appeal because they provide a temporary respite for consumers. Spending hard-earned cash on such necessities as food, housing and transport isn't nearly as much fun as spending it on something that literally has no value. There is an almost clandestine – and refreshing – feeling about it.

Do you think you could sell tinned London fog? One supersalesman has done just that. Another has made a tidy sum of money out of selling empty cardboard boxes. 'This box,' said the label, 'contains nothing for the person who has everything.' The contents, it added, were '100 per cent pure nothing – another quality product from the Rip-Off Corporation.'

The Great Chewing Gum Caper

One of the greatest salesmen of his day – and perhaps of all time – was William Wrigley Jr, who made more than $200 million out of chewing gum. No one needed chewing gum, but Wrigley, who boasted that he could sell pianos to the armless men of Borneo, persuaded countless Americans to buy it.

He had a great flair for dealing with people. Once, when he was still working as a soap salesman for his father's company, he won over a storekeeper (who had irritably criticized his selling technique) by asking for instruction in salesmanship, receiving it on the spot and getting an order for a year's supply of soap. When he started selling gum, he used every cent he had to mount the first spectacular advertising campaign in American history. A reporter who wanted to know his recipe for success was told: 'Get a good product. It's easier to row downstream than up. Then tell 'em quick, and tell 'em often . . . keep ever-lasting coming at them. Advertising is pretty much like running a train. Once you stop running, the fire goes out. The train will run on its own momentum for a while, but it will gradually slow down and come to a dead stop.'

Wrigley himself kept on stoking. As a result of one advertising contract, each of the 62,000 street, subway and elevated cars in America carried a Wrigley poster. His flashing electric sign in New York's Times Square cost $104,000 a year to run but reached millions. Along the Trenton-Atlantic City highway in the New Jersey meadows he erected an outdoor chain sign half a mile long advertising his products. He also mailed sample sticks of his gum to all 1.5 million subscribers then listed in America's telephone books, and sent more than 750,000 two-year-old children two sticks of gum every year on their birthdays. He even published Mother Goose books, rewritten to tie chewing gum into nursery jingles and dedicated 'to the children of the world – from 6 to 60'. Over a two-year period beginning in 1915 he distributed about 14 million of these. The rhymes were often crude but made their point:

> Jack be nimble
> Jack be quick
> Jack run and get your
> WRIGLEY stick!

> As I was going to St Ives
> I met a man with seven wives
> Each wife had a fine clear skin
> All were fat – not one was thin,
> And each had a dimple in her chin:
> What caused it? – WRIGLEY'S!

The books, written when relatively few were concerned with dieting, were filled with reminders that Wrigley gum steadied the nerves, sweetened the breath, soothed the throat, relieved thirst, quickened the appetite and aided digestion.

By 1930, Wrigley had factories everywhere. They were producing 40 million sticks of gum a day and his little green packages were printed in 37 languages. 'If Mr Wrigley has become one of the ten wealthiest millionaires in America, the *New Statesman* observed at the time, 'it is because humanity has instinctively recognized that he was helping to restore to it the lost art of chewing.'

Selling People

When Brian Epstein walked into a Liverpool cellar and saw a scruffy young group of pop singers in action for the first time, he could hardly have guessed that they would turn into one of the biggest money-spinners the music business has ever seen. The name of the group – the Beatles – certainly didn't sound like a winner. But he decided to take a chance and we all know the rest.

Selling people can be a highly lucrative business. This is particularly true of entertainers and sports personalities, who nowadays earn vast sums in a worldwide market – not only by performing but also by endorsing all kinds of products. John Travolta, for example, was paid $750,000 for saying just two words – 'Tokyo Drink' – in a Japanese 'TV commercial.

The trick is to find likely candidates for fame and to manage their careers in return for a percentage. The Hollywood star machine showed the way many years ago; television has widened the scope.

The Beatles, of course, were exceptional because they had a new kind of music and because John Lennon and Paul McCartney were uniquely talented songwriters. In the seven years before the group split up in 1970, they composed more than 200 songs, most of which are still played and sung today. Many other pop groups are nine-day wonders.

Talent-spotting is largely a matter of keeping one's eyes and ears open and of judging what – or who – is likely to appeal to the public. But it requires something more: the ability to persuade the right people to sign long-term contracts *before* they become stars and the supersalesman's knack of creating, developing and selling an image. Talent alone is seldom enough: a lot of capable performers never get anywhere. Skilful marketing is a vital part of a package. Look at Liberace: he was a good piano player, but he would never have reached super-stardom without those flashy sequin suits and ridiculous candelabra.

One of the most fascinating aspects of the game is the selling of politicians. Joseph Goebbels was an early (and evil) practitioner of the art: his propaganda skills played an immensely important role in the rise of Adolf Hitler. But even he, I fancy, would be amazed by the effort which now goes into creating and developing a vote-winning image. No American politician, however brilliant, can hope to become President without the help of supersalesmen and vast budgets. Other countries may spend less, but every party has acquired its own team of marketing experts: they have become an integral part of the democratic process.

Ronald Reagan's extraordinary transition from cowboy actor to Governor of California and then President owes much to expert salesmanship. There may be cleverer politicians in America, but few can match his marketing skill. As one well-known commentator has put it: 'Ronald Reagan will almost certainly go down as a great president, not for what he has done, but for the spirit he has embodied: the revival of Norman Rockwell American decency; the nicest of nice guys, the cheerful patriarch whom any American would feel perfectly at ease with around the supper table. Who cares that he sometimes seems unable to get what the Beirut thing, or the deficit thing, or the arms control thing, is all about? Nor can most of his fellow-countrymen.'

The message is plain: selling a politician works best if one concentrates on basics and ignores the small print. Personality rates above policies; slogans are more effective than well-informed (but long-winded) speeches. A politician's style is remembered long after everything else is forgotten.

'Ron' (as he calls himself in letters to other world leaders) is a salesman's dream come true. He has an instinctive feel for the market, knows how to deliver someone else's lines and rarely steps out of character. His image is sharply focused. People would certainly buy a used car from *this* man.

Other presidents have had to be more carefully packaged. One of John Kennedy's problems, early in his campaign, was that people thought he was too rich to understand the needs of ordinary people. So his sales team persuaded him to dress in blue jeans and frayed sneakers and to pose for endless pictures in hamburger joints and pizza parlours. Richard Nixon used the vice-presidency to bait 'Commies' but played down his tough guy image by being as folksy as a Sears Roebuck catalogue. When his opponents accused him of misdemeanour he went on television and made an emotional speech about his little dog. (Even the dog, though, couldn't save him after Watergate.) Jimmy Carter was portrayed as a God-fearing peanut farmer and amateur carpenter who, like little George Washington, could never tell a lie.

Here are some simple but important rules to keep in mind if you should ever find yourself involved in political salesmanship.

Establish a brand image

Don't confuse the public: people like their leaders to have an easily recognizable brand image. Judge the public's mood and make sure your candidate is right for it. There are dozens of options: decent Ron, honest Jimmy, folksy Dick, lovable Ike, tough Lyndon, vigorous Jack, caring Neil, fearless Ted, patriotic Margaret, and so on.

Self-made men are popular in America (less so in Britain) but don't allow your client to brag about his wealth: envy costs votes.

Clever people are generally disliked, so if you are stuck with an intellectual make sure he doesn't come across as arrogant.

Check his past

Politicians can't afford to have skeletons in their closets – or mistresses in their beds. A vigilant (and often hypocritical) press will eagerly demolish the reputation of anyone who is thought to have misbehaved. Divorce is acceptable (Ronald Regan was divorced) but affairs are not. Financial set-backs are forgiven, but involvement in some question-able business deal is disastrous. Make certain, before you agree to help, that there are unlikely to be any embarras-sing surprises.

Beware of humour

A ready smile is as important to a politician as it is to every other salesman, but a sense of humour can be dangerous. Funny politicians tend not to be taken seriously. By all means, encourage your client to make jokes at the expense of his opponents, but don't let him ridicule the ideas and values of the people who are supposed to vote for him.

Keep it simple

Plain English is essential for success: the politician who rambles on about the money supply and the balance of payments will never make it to the top. Bold, attention-grabbing speeches are most likely to keep your man – or woman – in the public eye. Get an advertising copywriter to write the speeches and draft some headline material for use at press conferences. Keep it simple – and say it often.

Send him on a world tour

A standard ploy which nearly always produces good results is to send an ambitious politician on a world tour, so that he can have his picture taken with presidents, prime ministers and royalty. This establishes him as a man of consequence, a potential statesman.

Get him on TV

Television is every politician's favourite platform, but it has to be carefully handled. It is all too easy to appear pompous, woolly, shifty, indecisive. A good performer comes across as sincere (even if he isn't) and authoritative. The people who can always count on getting invitations to appear on programmes are those who make crisp, provocative statements.

The value of gimmicks

If you are selling entertainers, gimmicks can be immensely helpful. I have already mentioned Liberace's candelabra; there are numerous other examples. The Beatles had identical clothes and haircuts. Yul Brynner and Telly Savalas achieved fame by shaving their heads. Jack Benny had his violin. Dean Martin walks on stage with a glass in his hand and plays the role of the amiable drunk. A gimmick which becomes a familiar trademark keeps the image in focus.

A variation of this is to devise a label which the media can use – Green Goddess, Golden Girl and so on. It greatly improves the chances that producers and advertising agencies will think of your client when they need someone for a lucrative job.

The showbiz world likes to put performers into clearly defined categories, and there is obviously much to be said for doing the same. If your client has a particular talent – if he is, say, a good rock musician – this is a simple matter. But if he is just another actor it pays to make sure that the public knows where it stands. The late John Wayne was not particularly talented or handsome, but he became enormously successful because he had the good sense to recognize the value of type-casting. Here are some of the most popular categories:

The good guy

Good guys used to deal with cattle rustlers and Nazi regiments; today they are more likely to tackle drug pushers, terrorists and communist spies. In comedies, they struggle to survive in a cruel world. The good guy can earn a lot of money in advertising because millions like to think that they are just like him. Good guys buy their wives chocolates and perfume, drive family cars, drink lager, save and never leave home without their American Express card.

The bad guy

Bad guys are harder to sell to advertisers, for obvious reasons, but they can count on steady employment in films and TV series. Some do extremely well. Larry Hagman (a charming fellow in private life) is instantly recognized all over the world as the scheming JR of *Dallas*; he and his manager must be laughing all the way to the bank.

The bitch

Joan Collins may resent the fact that so many people confuse fiction with reality, but playing the bitch has made her a fortune. Advertising agencies think she is marvellous. She is paid about $90,000 for each episode of *Dynasty*; advertising contracts, spin-off promotions and other perks bring her total income to something like $6 million a year. Bitches wear diamonds and expensive clothes, chain-smoke, fly first class and live in fancy apartments.

The hell-raiser

Errol Flynn was the archetypal hell-raiser: a mediocre actor who became famous because of his boisterous life-style. Hell-raisers can still count on getting ample publicity, even if they haven't made a film for years. They drive fast cars and drink gallons of Scotch.

The sex symbol

Hollywood's salesmen invented the sex symbol and made billions. The term sounds a bit old-fashioned in the 1980s but continues to be widely used. Female sex symbols can earn huge fees by promoting fur coats, jewellery, underwear and perfume. Male sex symbols appear in advertisements for vodka and bourbon, watches, sports clothes, pyjamas, sunglasses, airlines and after-shave lotion.

First steps

Mark McCormack, whose International Management Group represents more than 500 clients and has a turnover of $200 million a year, started his business in the 1960s with a capital of under $500. He was, at the time, a young lawyer with a passion for gold and he decided that one way of combining business with pleasure was to represent promising players. His first three clients – Arnold Palmer, Gary Player and Jack Nicklaus – became big names with his help.

People now tell him that he was 'lucky' and he concedes that luck played an important role. He was indeed fortunate to find three talented players who not only became stars but dominated the game for a decade. But you don't build up a business on luck alone: good judgment, determination and a willingness to take risks are equally important. McCormack went on to extend his activities to other areas, such as tennis and Grand Prix racing.

There is clearly much to be said for concentrating, in the early stages, on a field you know well and creating a stable of potential winners. Look for people who are likely to have staying power; you don't want to be saddled with a nine-day wonder. When you have found them, make sure they sign an airtight contract and treat them fairly: you don't want to lose them just when you have managed to turn them into hot properties.

The Swapping Game

If you were selling, say, steam turbines to Romania and they offered to pay you in *nails*, what would be your response?

The supersalesmen at General Electric, who faced that problem, did not hesitate. They took the nails.

Barter may strike you as ludicrously old-fashioned, but it has been making a big comeback. There is a new, more dignified term for it: counter-trade.

The revival started when communist countries, always notoriously short of hard currency, insisted on paying for Western goods in kind. The West didn't like the idea at all, but saying 'no' would have meant losing sales. So General Electric settled for nails, and McDonell Douglas sold jets to Yugoslavia for meat and to Poland for leather coats, canned hams, men's wallets, hand tools and power transmission lines.

In recent years counter-trade has also become increasingly popular with Third World countries, especially those with debt problems, to the extent that Latin America, Africa and Asia have now overtaken Eastern Europe in this type of business.

Two examples: Chrysler has sold trucks to Jamaica in exchange for alumina, and Caterpillar Tractor has swapped earth-moving equipment for Algerian wine.

Counter-trade is a blanket term; there are actually several varieties.

There is the straightforward *barter* deal, where one type of product is simply exchanged for another.

Counter-purchase is where an exporter agrees to *buy*

goods and services from the country he is selling to. There are two parallel but separate contracts: one for the first order and one for the counter-purchase. The value of the counter-purchase ranges from 10 per cent to 100 per cent or more of the original export order. This is the most common type of counter-trade.

Buy-back, a form of barter, is favoured by the Soviet Union. Suppliers of capital plant or equipment agree to be paid in the future by the output of the factory they are supplying. A few years ago a top British construction firm sold an irrigation system to the Romanians and was paid in produce subsequently grown, which was then sold in Brazil for cash.

Offset is where an exporter incorporates into his product something that is manufactured in the importing country.

Switch-trading is where a Western exporter is paid by a third country which has a trade deficit with the importer.

A few large exporters can generally handle all the trans-actions themselves, but smaller ones have to go to counter-

---

We're all familiar with the basic forms of barter – trading in an old car for a new one, for example.

But the practice can sometimes create baffling problems for the uninitiated.

Take the heart-rending predicament which faced Mademoiselle Zélie of the Théâtre Lyrique of Paris when her fee for a concert in one of the Society Islands turned out to be 3 pigs, 23 turkeys, 44 chickens, all distinctly alive; 5,000 coconuts and considerable quantities of bananas, lemons and oranges.

What was a Parisian artiste, half-way around the world from home, a prima donna without refrigeration or a sense of humour, to do with all that stuff? Set up a market stall? Swap that lot for a boat which would get her out of there the next day? What would *you* have done?

---

trading specialists. These are either fully fledged trading companies, which take on counter-purchase obligations and then sell onto the end-user, or they are advisory departments of banks.

Counter-trading can be a time-consuming, costly and uncertain method of trading. But it often makes all the difference between success and failure.

Finding
Customers

How to be a Good Prospector

Supersalesmen do not trudge from door to door. Nor do they thumb through the Yellow Pages in a desperate effort to find people to call on. They aim high and they choose their targets carefully.

Prospecting – the search for potential buyers – is basic to all selling. Some people do it better than others: they are the salesmen who end up with the biggest cheques. If you devote all your time to maintaining old accounts, you will make little progress. Indeed, you may slip back. Some customers may leave the company they work for, some will switch to another supplier, some will go out of business, and some will find that they no longer need your product. To move forward, you must get more buyers – and to do *that* you must discover new prospects.

One of the most obvious ways of doing so is to ask a customer who is satisfied with your product if he knows others who might be interested. People generally do; they may even agree to write a letter, or make a phone call, on your behalf.

Another method, sometimes called 'bird-dogging', is to develop a list of contacts who will feed you with names. They may be professional people, like lawyers and bank managers, who deal with a lot of businessmen and, in the course of doing so, learn a great deal about their needs. They may even be other salesmen, working in non-competing fields. If they know that you will pay them a commission, or return the favour at some future date, they will often be glad to steer you in the right direction.

The supersalesman is constantly on the alert for leads. He has a 'nose for business' which enables him to spot opportunities wherever, and whenever, they may arise. He does not confine his prospecting to office hours because he knows that valuable information can come to him at any time. It may be an item in a newspaper or an interview on television. It may be a comment made by an old, or new, acquaintance over lunch or at a cocktail party. It may be a hint dropped by someone he meets on a racecourse, at a golf club, on a sailing weekend, at a wedding, and even at a funeral.

It helps, of course, if you move in the right circles. A salesman who spends most of his time in the company of his own kind may have a lot of fun, but he is more likely to meet worthwhile prospects if he makes a point of cultivating influential people.

Where to meet the right people

On Concorde   Concorde is the nearest thing to an airborne club of the rich and successful. It is the natural habitat of the supersalesman, who knows that a casual chat with the man in the next seat could lead to a deal worth millions.

If you have to take a subsonic flight, always go first class. You can't afford to let people think that you are doing badly, and you won't find many chairmen or chief executives in Economy.

In smart restaurants   Supersalesmen don't go to fashionable (and invariably over-priced) restaurants because of the food, which is often inferior to that served in less expensive establishments. They go there to meet influential contacts, initiate and close deals, or simply to be seen by people who matter.

The private dining-rooms of banks and other institutions are also useful, not only because your fellow guests may well include a leading industrialist, Government official, or

politician, but also because they present an ideal opportunity to sell your latest project to people who are in a
position to provide the necessary financial backing.

If you can't procure an invitation to one of these cosy
sessions, start your own dining club in the office or in a
private room at a smart restaurant. Use prominent personalities as bait. People will always come to hear the views of an
important speaker, and your motive will be less obvious.
You will, of course, have to pay him a fee, but if it enables
you to lure a dozen good prospects to your table it will be a
worthwhile investment.

At conferences and seminars   Only the innocent go to
conferences and seminars to hear the speeches. Supersalesmen use them to pick the brains of other salesmen, or
to trap rivals into making indiscreet revelations, or to meet
new prospects.

The annual meetings of the International Monetary Fund
and the World Bank attract a large number of bankers and
other middle-men. Few bother to attend the sessions themselves; they are there because they see these meetings as a
heaven-sent opportunity to talk business with the finance
ministers and officials of many countries. In other words,
they are prospecting.

Countless other events which are billed as festivals and
fairs are, in reality, excuses for hectic horse-trading. The
Cannes Film Festival is a notable example.

Seminars are used in the same way as private luncheon
clubs. Prospects are ostensibly invited to hear an interesting speech, but the real purpose is to make contact with
potential customers. I am often asked to speak at seminars
for insurance brokers, fund managers and computer users.
It is well-paid work, and I do my best to please, but I am well
aware that these occasions are thinly disguised exercises in
salesmanship.

Sometimes the organizers don't bother with the disguise.

Only the innocent go to hear the speeches.

One insurance company which asked me to chair a series of seminars sent out invitations with a message with far more pulling power than my name could ever hope to have: 'Come to hear how you can get your share of £2 billion.' The company was selling a new pension scheme to insurance brokers and the response was tremendous. I was merely there to provide a little entertainment.

At cocktail parties and receptions   Supersalesmen do not give parties so that people can have fun – though some guests manage to do just that. The principal purpose is to bring together people who are likely to be useful to them. Social functions enable them to engage in seemingly idle chat with prospects and to follow it up with a telephone call the next day. It helps, of course, if one can attract a few well-known personalities. Royals are best, but television news-readers and chat show hosts can also help to give the entirely spurious impression that there is no ulterior motive.

Supersalesmen also hire boxes for famous racing occasions like Ascot and the Derby, and buy Centre Court seats for Wimbledon, so that they can entertain their more promising prospects. Business may or may not be discussed on these occasions, but you may be sure that it will be discussed afterwards. There is no such thing as a free box or Centre Court seat, just as there is no such thing as a free lunch.

At the very top, a lot of entertaining is done in splendid country houses or on the company yacht. This is where the banker or the company chairman who is chasing a fat contract has a quiet chat, over the brandy and cigars, with an Arab prince or a Minister in charge of one of the big spending departments. They like to pretend that they are not selling – they are merely 'talking about subjects of mutual interest' – but no one is really fooled. They are simply engaging in high-level salesmanship: the method may be different, but the aim is the same.

If you happen to be a fellow-guest on one of these occasions, remember that it is considered bad form to muscle in on the host's game. He is, after all, footing the bill. But there is no reason why you should not approach the prospect, after a suitable interval, and suggest that you, too, would like to talk about 'subjects of mutual interest'.

Screening Prospects

It is not, of course, enough to have a list of prospects. There is another important step before one can attempt to turn them into customers: they must be qualified, or screened.

All salesmen realize the importance of prospecting, but many lack the ability to make a proper evaluation. An awful lot of time is wasted on chasing people who, for one reason or another, are unlikely to buy.

Supersalesmen generally have a 'sixth sense' which helps them to size up a prospect. But they do not rely on instinct alone. They try to find out as much as possible about him or her before taking the next step. The more information you have, the better your chances of success. If really big money is involved, it usually pays to get someone to make a thorough (but discreet) investigation and prepare a dossier which will give you most, if not all, the details you need before making your approach. In screening a prospect, you have to ask yourself four basic questions.

Is he a decision-maker?

People may show keen interest in your product or service, but that won't get you very far if they lack the authority to make buying decisions or, at least, to influence them. So try to discover who has the clout before you go any further. This is comparatively easy with small companies: the key decisions are invariably made by the chairman and/or managing director. Large organizations are more complex. The top man may give you a sympathetic hearing, and may even show enthusiasm, but he won't necessarily make the decision. If he has delegated authority, he will be reluctant to interfere. He should be able to steer you in the right direction, but don't assume that his support will guarantee success and don't make the mistake of using his name in a way which could be regarded as arrogant. It will simply produce resentment.

If you don't know anyone in the organization, call the department which is most likely to be interested in your product or service and find out who's in charge. Friendly enquiries among staff (especially secretaries) will often tell you all you need to know.

Is there a want or need?

It obviously helps if you can establish that the prospect has a need or want for what you have to sell. He may not recognize the need – it's up to you to convince him. What counts is your assessment of the situation. If he has already bought all the modern office equipment he can possibly use there isn't much point in asking him to buy still more. If he has just taken delivery of a new Rolls-Royce or a Cadillac he is unlikely to want another. And so on.

GETTING THE MAIL READ

If you are corresponding with someone on a regular basis, and you know each other well, he or she is sure to read your letter. The same, alas, is not necessarily true of mail sent to a prospect you have never met before. People today are bombarded with junk mail, and most of it isn't even looked at before it's thrown away. This is why so many expensive direct mail campaigns produce such poor returns.

Sending your letter to the prospect's home address, rather than the office, may improve your chances of getting it read, but even that is by no means guaranteed. Too many other salesmen are already doing just that, and many people are annoyed by what they regard as an intrusion on their privacy.

Marking the envelope 'personal and confidential' is another ploy which is likely to irritate the recipient if it turns out that it is just another piece of promotional material.

Here is how you can improve the odds:

Write a genuine letter, instead of sending printed stuff.

Don't use your company's name on the outside of the envelope, or do anything which identifies it as advertising mail. Don't show your hand; use plain envelopes and first-class postage.

If you do send printed material, enclose a short personal note. Say: 'I thought this might interest you.'

Don't sell *too* hard. Short 'soft-sell' messages are often more effective. If the prospect has done business with you before, send him a card at Christmas and, if possible, for his birthday. Calendars are also useful; they will put your name in front of the customer all year long.

If you are sending promotional material to his office, address it to his secretary rather than the great man himself and ask her to bring it to his attention. She will be flattered that you have taken the trouble to find out her name and that you regard her as influential.

Making that little extra effort may be time-consuming and costly, but 100 well-aimed and carefully written pieces of mail often produce better results than 1,000 pieces of junk.

Can he afford to pay?

It is equally useless to sell someone on the need for your product and then learn that he has cash-flow problems or that his credit is bad. It isn't always possible to get this information before calling on a prospect, but one should try. Enquiries among his customers may provide a clue (though one should beware of mischievous rumours) and there are credit-rating sources, such as Dun and Bradstreet, which can be consulted. If he is running a public company, a copy of the latest report and accounts may be helpful.

Is the time right?

However much a prospect may like your product, he may be unwilling or unable to buy at this particular time. He may be going through a lean period, or his budget may be fully committed. If you make your proposal at the wrong moment, you are liable to get a negative response, regardless of its merits. You can, of course, try to create a relationship which will enable you to come back, and make the sale, when conditions are more favourable. But if you want to make the most effective use of your own time it is more sensible to concentrate on people who are likely to want your product *now*.

Selling on the Telephone

The telephone can be a salesman's best friend – if it's used properly. It generates instant response, costs less than face-to-face meetings and reduces the risk of misunderstanding. It widens your market, saves time and allows you to 'qualify' prospects before you take the next step.

Many salesmen, nevertheless, dislike it intensely. This is largely because they feel, not without reason, that a 'cold call' is an intrusion which invites a rude reply. It is hard to maintain your enthusiasm if the first ten people you phone say: 'I haven't got time to talk to salesmen' or 'Why are you bothering me?' Prospecting by telephone is uphill work. But it can also produce good results and no salesman worth his commission can afford to ignore its merits.

A common mistake is to think in terms of the number of calls. The number of calls made in a day is not important: what counts is getting through to the right person, discovering whether he or she has any interest, and making a sale or at least securing an appointment. To achieve this you have to do a little homework; simply picking up the telephone and calling people at random is doing it the hard way. Try to identify the people who matter, be sure to say something to arouse their interest and choose a good time to call. Don't be discouraged by the occasional rudeness – it isn't personal and you haven't really done them any harm. You can always say: 'I'm sorry I disturbed you. Goodbye.'

A lot, of course, depends on *what* you are selling. If you are, say, an advertising representative of a newspaper or magazine it is common practice to call an agency and make your pitch. Other fields, such as life insurance, tend to be more difficult. The mere mention of the word 'insurance' turns many people off. The principal objective here is to set up a meeting, so that you can make a personal presentation, and the way to do that is to offer a benefit. Say: 'I would appreciate a few minutes of your time to show you how you can reduce taxes.' Or: 'I have a proposal which I think you will find is just right for your company.'

Getting past screeners

Most executives have someone who screens their calls, generally a private secretary. She has to be convinced that he will want to talk to you. If you are 'maintenance selling' – serving existing customers – that shouldn't present any great problem. But if neither she nor he has ever heard of you he will almost certainly be much harder to reach.

Some salesmen resort to silly tricks, like pretending to be the family doctor or lawyer. It may just possibly get them past the screen, but it invariably produces an angry reaction when the executive discovers that it is a lie. Few people find that kind of thing funny. Another ploy is to claim that you are a 'personal friend'. But a good secretary will always check, and if her boss replies, 'Never heard of him,' she will naturally assume that you are a charlatan.

A title is helpful, and you can always make one up. 'Colonel Smith' or even 'Sir John Smith' as I have said before, sounds much more impressive than plain John Smith. Again, though, there is an obvious risk that your deception will backfire.

It is simpler, and certainly more honest, to project confidence and authority. Avoid anything that will typecast you as 'just another salesman'; imply vaguely that what you have to say is important. Say: 'My name is John Smith of Consolidated. I would like to speak to Mr Brown, please.' Don't go into detail; she is not the decision-maker. She may ask: 'Does he know you?' Tell her: 'We haven't met, but I am sure

Mr Brown is familiar with my company and will be very interested in what I have to say. Would you tell him that I am on the phone, please?' If you can mention the name of a third party who is known to him or her, so much the better.

She may, of course, use the standard excuse that 'he's in a meeting' – which may or may not be true. Leave a message which indicates that the matter you wish to discuss is of some consequence. He will probably be intrigued. If he does not return your call, don't hesitate to call again. This time ask the secretary her name and *use* it. Say: 'Miss Jones, Mr Brown and I both have very busy schedules. Is there any particular time when it would be best to call? Is three o'clock all right or would you suggest four o'clock?' This conveys that you, too, are a man whose time is valuable and may persuade her to make a commitment.

If you still get an evasive answer when you call at the suggested time, you may be tempted to give up. Don't. He will probably talk to you if you persist, either because you have managed to arouse his curiosity or simply in order to be rid of you.

Some people start work very early, before secretaries and other staff get to the office, and have no choice but to answer the phone themselves. Others work late, and the security guard (who has no experience at screening phone calls) will put you through.

A phone call in non-business hours, late at night or at weekends, always has greater impact. But it is not recommended if you are merely trying to sell him something which should properly be discussed in the office. Such calls work only if you know him socially, or if you are proposing a deal which is of personal advantage to him and must, therefore, be discussed in private. Real estate agents generally have a good excuse. They may call to say: 'Sorry to trouble you, but we have an excellent property in the area which has just come on the market at a very advantageous price. We felt that you might want to know. Would you be interested in buying it, if we also handled the sale of your present home? Or do you know someone who might be interested?' Many people switch homes quite often and seldom resent an effort to make them aware of good opportunities.

Getting attention

Once you have made contact with the prospect, you must quickly arouse his interest to *keep* him on the telephone. He can easily hang up. Don't waste his time with chit-chat about the weather. If you have a mutual friend or acquaintance, start by mentioning his name – 'Jack Collins suggested that I should call you.' If not, get directly to the point – which is that you have something to offer that will be of benefit to him.

A technique used by some salesmen is the 'market survey routine'. You call and say: 'We are doing a market survey; is it all right if I ask you a few questions?' He may be flattered that you have singled him out for attention, and may well agree to see you so that you can go into more detail.

Don't be subservient: confidence and an air of authority are just as important in dealing with him as in getting past the screener. And don't give him too much information. The aim is not to get him to make a hasty decision (which is quite likely to be negative) but to get an appointment. Write a follow-up letter confirming the date and time.

How to Play Customer Golf

They do not, as far as I know, teach customer golf at business schools, but it can surely be only a matter of time before they do. Some corporations already employ vice-presidents whose main function is to play golf with the right people, and in the business world generally a handicap is increasingly regarded as an asset.

In the US and Japan, and to a growing extent in Europe, business and golf have become almost inseparable. Businessmen buy their way into a club – or let their companies do it for them – so that they can make contact with potential customers and humour existing ones.

A morning on the golf course is frequently more lucrative than a week at the office – and a lot more pleasant. In the office, businessmen are harassed, suspicious and over-cautious. If they run large corporations, they are also likely to be well protected by officious secretaries and personal assistants. On the golf course, they are relaxed, approachable and receptive. It is not really done to discuss business while you are swinging a club, but many deals have begun with a casual remark on the fairway.

Bankers, stockbrokers, insurance salesmen and advertising agencies have acquired some of their best clients while blasting out of a bunker, and many ambitious executives have managed to sell themselves to employers by subtly developing a golf partnership.

You can ring a partner up, a week later, and he will remember you. He may even invite you to his own home – where you will naturally do your best to impress him with

your arguments. Or he may call you, with a request that you should meet to discuss that casual remark.

There are, however, two basic rules which should never be broken. Don't be obvious. And don't try to do business with anyone who is having a bad game. Many a promising relationship has been destroyed by crassness. People have sidled up to golf partners and tried to borrow large sums of money. Or they have eagerly pushed forward major propositions at the most unsuitable moments. Ploys like this invariably turn out to be self-defeating. They cause embarrassment and give offence to other club members. The golf course is essentially a launching pad. It brings people together and allows them to plant ideas.

If you have trouble setting up an appointment, it may pay to arouse the prospect's curiosity by sending him a video tape of your standard presentation so that he can view it at home.

Many travel companies are doing just that: it has the merit of attracting the attention of the whole family. The technique can be used in numerous other fields, and there is nowadays a large number of professional organizations which can produce a first-class tape for you.

Audio cassettes are cheaper, but often just as effective. The prospect can play the cassette in his car, or office, or at home. Ask a satisfied customer if he will help you by recording an interview. Get him to say what a great job you have done, how happy he is with your product or service, and how much he has benefited from it. Praise from a customer always has more credibility than a straightforward sales pitch. It may not result in an immediate order, but at least it should get you past the door.

How to Make a
Good Presentation

Sell the Sizzle, not the Steak

Let us, before we go any further, establish a fundamental principle of good salesmanship. You don't sell a *thing*, you sell the *benefits* of a thing.

An employer will not hire you simply because he likes the colour of your eyes. He will do so because you have persuaded him that he needs you – that your services will boost his profits. The same applies to every product or service that one cares to mention. People will always buy the end result a lot faster than they'll buy the product or service itself. There are millions of telephones sold each year. No one wants a telephone but everyone wants the means of keeping in easy touch with others.

It is astonishing how often salesmen ignore this basic rule. They prattle on at irritating length about the technical aspects of a product and even try to gain the customer's sympathy by telling him: 'I need this order.' It may work in a few cases, but it is usually the wrong approach. *Your* needs are not important; **his** are.

The supersalesman recognizes this crucial fact and acts accordingly. He knows that a sale is made when the need or desire to own a product or to command a service is stronger than a buyer's natural instinct to hold on to his money. And he is good at making people *aware* of those needs and desires. There is a famous maxim which should hang on every salesman's office wall: 'Sell the sizzle, not the steak.' It's the sizzle that makes people's mouths water.

The buyer is always concerned with what he believes a product or service will do for him. A good computer salesman does not merely point out what a marvellous gadget he is offering. He succeeds because he manages to convince the buyer that it will make his job easier, reduce his costs and allow him to give a better service to his customers. A good insurance salesman does not confine himself to outlining the financial details of a scheme. He plays on emotional factors: the need to be secure, the desire to do the best for one's family. A good real estate salesman does not sell a house simply because it provides shelter. He stresses all the other aspects which he knows will trigger an emotional response: status, convenience, pleasure, and its value as an investment.

Buying motives vary, but psychologists have identified these basic 'impulses'.

Pride of ownership	Desire for gain
Vanity	Convenience
Self-preservation	Prestige and status
Ambition	Love of family
Avoidance of worry	Pleasure
Self-improvement	Fear of loss

The trick is to discover which of these is *dominant* in any particular situation, and the obvious way to do that is to ask a lot of questions – and do a lot of careful listening. Put yourself in the prospect's place: what would you do and how would you react if you were the buyer? There may or may not be a combination of motives, and quite often people will not give the *real* reason for their interest. A couple who buy a home in a fancy district may be reluctant to admit that they are primarily concerned with prestige and status, so they will tell you that 'it's convenient for the office' or 'it's a good area for the children'. A businessman who buys a new Rolls-Royce or Cadillac may *say* that he is doing so because it's needed, but there will almost certainly be additional motives.

You'll score time after time if you take the trouble to find out what really matters. Forget about your own tastes and preferences: they are immaterial. Your job is to establish what the prospect wants, re-inforce his desires and convince him or her that you have the best solution.

Be a Showman

When the late – and great – Walt Disney tried to sell a project to potential backers he frequently acted out his concepts and dialogues. It must have been a splendid sight to see him at work in some sceptical banker's office, playing all the parts in a Mickey Mouse or Donald Duck scenario.

Today he would almost certainly use a variety of modern visual aids, notably a video film. But the basic principle has remained the same: if you want to get attention, it pays to use showmanship.

There are, of course, supersalesmen who make vast deals by outlining a concept in a few sentences over a pleasant lunch. If you have a good track record, and the idea appeals to the prospect, you can often get agreement without preparing an elaborate presentation. Others can be left to take care of the details *after* you have sold the idea. But, as a general rule, customers expect to see evidence that you have done your homework and they are more likely to respond if you make an impact through the *eye* as well as the ear.

Busy people have short attention spans. If you make a long-winded verbal presentation they will probably let you finish (though prospects *have* been known to walk out half-way through, saying that they have another urgent meeting to go to) but your message may well fail to get through. Don't bore the prospect: engage his emotions. If a picture is worth 1,000 words, use it.

When an advertising agency sets out to win a new account it rarely relies on words alone. It will use flip charts, slides, artwork, films and whatever else is likely to appeal to the eye. People who are trained to visualize the end product may not need such elaborate aids, but the average business manager has to be *shown* what he is getting. I make a lot of presentations for new magazine projects, and I always include artwork or even a full-scale 'dummy' which gives the prospect a clear picture of what the magazine will *look* like.

If you are selling expensive industrial equipment, models can be very helpful. You can also make your audience sit up by showing how your product works in practice. Salesmen working for one big American paper company invariably bring in an unusual mechanical device which dramatically tests the strength of their product. When a lever is tripped, a steel ball, three inches in diameter, drops on a sheet of paper made by a competitor and breaks through it. When a similar sheet made by the company is placed on the holder, and the ball is dropped, there is no damage. Simple but effective.

It does not, of course, mean that words are unimportant. The prospect will still want to know all the relevant details, especially costs. But visual aids will strengthen your case. They will also allow you to deliver more information in less time. A lively, stimulating half-hour presentation, delivered with enthusiasm and backed up by appropriate slides or film, is likely to produce better results than an hour-long talk. It requires more effort, and is more expensive, but it is usually a worthwhile investment. What you are selling, essentially, is a concept that appeals to the imagination. If the prospect likes it, he will ask you to elaborate. If you fail to capture his imagination, he will thank you politely and find some excuse for saying 'no'.

What a good presentation must do

A good presentation is designed from the *buyer's* point of view. It must show what the product or service will do for him. Your proposals must fit into his business; don't ask him to fit his business into your proposition. The presentation must be believed, agreed with and acted upon.

It must be clearly understood

Don't get too technical. Most people don't want to hear all the technical details; they want to know what *benefits* your product or service will bring them. Don't talk over their heads.

If the prospects are knowledgeable themselves, they will be irritated by a presentation which contains a mass of information which they are already familiar with. Let them ask technical questions if they wish: if they don't, concentrate only on the end result.

A good presentation is clearly understood. Don't rely on the prospect to remember all the key points: sum up at the end. A popular clergyman once explained the secret of his powerful sermons like this: 'First, I tell them what I'm going to tell them. Second, I tell them. Third, I quickly tell them what I told them.' It is the outline of all successful speeches and sales presentations. You don't have to say exactly the same thing three times, but there is much to be said for skilful repetition.

Bring the customer into the act

A good salesman will always try to get the prospect involved. If he is selling clothes, he will urge him to 'feel the material' or to 'look at the workmanship'. If he is selling a car, he will invite him to take it for a test drive. In a formal presentation, he will allow him to handle the product or encourage him to comment on what is being said. Don't do *all* the talking.

Mention past successes

If your product or service has a good track record, say so. Many people rely heavily on the experience of others, and a satisfied customer is your best advertisement. But don't overdo it. The prospect is chiefly interested in how you can help him to achieve *his* objectives. Personalize your presentation: convey the impression that, whatever else you may have done before, *this* proposal is tailor-made for him.

The Power of Words

It helps, of course, if you have mastered the art of using the right words at the right time. Some salesmen never get the hang of it. Careless with language, and insensitive to the moods of others, they find themselves rejected with alarming frequency and never quite seem to grasp why they are less successful than others. Words create mental images, arouse emotions and cause things to happen. The wrong words, used at the wrong time, produce a negative response, even if the product is all that it should be. Here are some basic rules.

Appeal to the prospect's self-interest

Words like 'you' and 'yours' are always preferable to 'I' (and that very English term, 'one') because they are more likely to command attention. We don't want to hear salesmen talking about themselves – we want to know what they can do for us. If you are selling a house (for example) the most successful approach is likely to be one with direct appeals to the prospect's self-interest. 'Your new home in the country' has a better chance of producing a positive response than the impersonal 'a home in the country'.

Be sincere

Avoid shopworn words and phrases which sound insincere. 'Have a nice day!' may have been a pleasing expression when it was first used, but today it tends to be delivered with such mechanical frequency that it has become meaningless. And few things are more irritating than the equally mechanical assurance, when you shop for a new suit or a jacket, that 'it really looks good on you'. Many salesmen say it about everything you try on, sometimes without even bothering to look. It *may* produce a quick sale, but if the prospect has been pressured into making a bad buy he will avoid your shop in future. The supersalesman *always* appears to be genuinely interested in doing his best for the customer.

Use positive words

Don't use words which raise doubts in the prospect's mind or which imply that you are not sure of your own product or about your ability to deliver. 'Later' and 'perhaps' are two obvious examples. People like you to do things for them *now*, not later. And they don't want to be told that you *may* be able to deliver; words like 'certainly' and 'of course' are more likely to lead to a sale. Positive words trigger the right emotional response; negative words invariably have the opposite effect. Look at my list of strong and weak words and ask yourself which have the best chance of getting a positive reaction from *you*.

Avoid scare words

A scare word is any term which creates fear and which reminds the prospect that you are trying to sell something to him or her. The usual response is that dreaded phrase: 'I'll think about it.'

A typical scare word is 'sign'. A lot of people hate being asked to sign anything, because they are afraid of what they might be getting into. If you need someone's signature, use alternative terms which are less worrying. Ask them to 'OK the paperwork' or to 'approve the form'. Try to avoid any mention of the word 'contract', with its implied threat that, if things go wrong, the customer will end up in court. Call it 'agreement' or 'the paperwork'.

Another scare word is 'cost'. You can hardly avoid telling

the prospect, at some point or other, what he is going to have to pay for his purchase. But don't do it until you have created enthusiasm for your product or service, and try to use words which will make him feel happier about spending all that money. If you are selling a house or an insurance policy, call it an 'investment'. If you are selling a car or a mink coat, don't say: 'It costs £10,000.' Any of these words are better:

> Valued at
> Worth
> Available for
> Offered for

Remember that most people don't want to buy, they just want to own. Anything which takes the sting out of the need to part with their cash improves your chances of making a sale.

Go easy on the jargon

There are times when the use of jargon may be necessary – in selling to experts, for example. But as a general rule it pays to keep things simple.

We live, alas, in an age in which jargon is proliferating at an alarming rate. At one time only lawyers and bureaucrats seemed determined to murder English; now there are assassination squads all over the place. Much of the fancy talk is ugly and gets in the way of understanding. It's hard to get a positive emotional response if people don't know what the hell you are talking about.

Take insurance. Faced with words like 'maturity', 'indemnity', 'loading surrender', 'terminal bonus', and 'decreasing whole life with-profit policy', the man or woman in the street is not only confused but has the uneasy feeling that he or she is being conned. Lack of adequate communication breeds suspicion, and suspicion leads to hostility.

The salesman who cannot translate such terms into plain English is all too likely to go away empty-handed.

The computer industry is just as bad. There may not be a problem when you are selling to people whose job it is to understand these things, but if you are trying to convince an ordinary couple that they can't live without a home computer there is no point in dazzling them (or, for that matter, the average business manager) with a lot of jargon.

In most cases, the use of plain English – language that appeals to the heart as well as the head – is not only more attractive but also makes sound commercial sense.

Strong	**Weak**
Sure	Assume
Value	Perhaps
Special	Likely
Opportunity	Later
New	Some time
Executive	Slow
Certain	Small
Reliable	Guess
Wonderful	Sorry
Now	Suppose
Exciting	Don't know
Super	Poor
Happy	Old
Winner	Doubtful
Today	Risk
Big	Probably
Asset	Difficult
Good	Down
Remarkable	Ordinary
Best	Adequate
Benefit	Problem

Writing Letters

Many salesmen hate writing letters – and, for that matter, reports and memos. They regard it as an irksome chore. But, of course, it is very much part of business life, so you should really try to make the best of a necessary job. Supersalesmen invariably write good letters.

Take a look at your own mail and assess your response. What kind of letter makes a favourable impression on you? What kind turns you off? The chances are that they will have the same effect on others. Then take a critical look at the letters *you* have written in the past week and ask yourself, honestly, how well they compare with the ones that impressed you. If they don't measure up, change your style. Writing isn't difficult. You can learn to write as easily as you learned to talk. The starting point is to do just that – write as you talk.

Dos and don'ts

Don't use stiff and formal phrases. Don't start your letter with old-fashioned expressions like 'In reference to your communication of . . .' Say: 'Thank you for your letter of . . .' Be direct and use friendly, not formal, words.

Bad	**Good**
At the present time	Now
Prior to	Before
Request	Ask
Assistance	Help
Dispatched	Sent

As a result of	Because
This is to advise you	We are pleased to tell you
In addition	Also
In the event that	If

Don't write long, rambling letters. Be as concise as you can: the recipient's time is as valuable as yours. Lord Beaverbrook used to tell his journalists: 'Keep your sentences short, keep your paragraphs short, and capture the reader's interest right at the start. Don't bury your main point in a mass of detail.' It was good advice.

Don't be obsequious. People like to be treated with respect, but servility is a turn-off. You may be able to get away with it in face-to-face meetings, but in a letter it is clearly to be seen what it is: bullshit. A prime example is the dated English custom of ending letters with 'I remain, sir, your obedient servant.' No one believes, today, that you are *anyone's* obedient servant. A simple 'Yours sincerely' has much more credibility.

Don't be too familiar. A letter addressed to the recipient by name is more likely to be read than one which opens with 'Dear Sir or Madam'. But be careful about calling people you hardly know by their first name. Some businessmen don't mind; others find it impertinent. Even worse is the English public school practice (now, happily, dying out) of addressing someone only by his surname. 'Dear Davis' is pompous and offensive.

Do get the recipient's name and title right. Elementary – but a surprisingly large number of letters are ruined because the recipient's name is misspelled or because insufficient trouble has been taken to check the title. People are very touchy about these things and a wrongly addressed letter, no matter how well written, can do more harm than good. Make absolutely sure your secretary understands how important this is; if there is the slightest doubt, get her to check.

Do go easy on the exclamation marks. Some salesmen pepper their letters with ! and even !!!! It is generally quite unjustified and, if used to excess, extremely irritating. It also tends to be counter-productive: you lay yourself open to a charge of over-selling. Exclamation marks should be used only to stress something which is *truly* significant.

Don't make misleading statements. It is one thing to exaggerate in conversation; it is quite another to do so in a letter. Written claims and promises may be used against you if things go wrong.

The Moment of
Truth

The Close

Every salesman knows the feeling. You have made your presentation, the prospect is still awake, and he hasn't looked at his watch for the last fifteen minutes. He has asked some pertinent questions that clearly indicate interest, but he hasn't reached for his cheque-book.

It is at this point – the moment of truth – that many salesmen lose their nerve. They know that they *ought* to be asking for the order, but they are afraid to do so. What if he says 'no'? Wouldn't it be better to go over it all again, or perhaps say that you will call him next week?

They are almost relieved when the prospect says that he will 'think it over' because it has saved them from having to press for a decision. It shows, they think, that the presentation has been successful – the prospect merely needs more time to consider the proposal.

The supersalesman knows better. Prospects who say they will 'think it over' and promise to be 'in touch' tend to forget all about your proposition. They move on to other things. When you call a week later they will probably fob you off with something like 'We haven't had time to discuss it yet' or, more likely, 'We have given it careful consideration but we feel that it wouldn't be right to go ahead right now.' There is nothing you can do about it; the sale is lost.

The truth is that most prospects *expect* to be asked for an order at the end of a presentation. If they didn't, they wouldn't have agreed to see you. If you are nervous and hesitant, your lack of confidence will make a bad impression. It suggests that you don't have any real faith in your product or service, and produces doubt in the prospect's mind.

It is, of course, entirely possible that his answer will be 'no'. You will naturally be disappointed, but don't automatically assume that it is the prospect's last word. You may simply have to do a bit more selling. Many successful salesmen work on the principle that 'the sale doesn't begin until the customer says "no"'. It may be an exaggeration, but persistence pays off in a surprisingly large number of cases. You *may* have to ask three or four times before you get a positive answer.

Most people find it easier to say 'no' than 'yes'. This is particularly true of executives in large companies, who tend to operate on the principle that 'if you don't stick your neck out, it can't be chopped off'. But it also applies to individuals acting on their own behalf. They may be tempted to buy, but are afraid to enter into new commitments.

The supersalesman knows how to distinguish between a firm 'no' – one which is clearly the final word – and a hesitant one, based chiefly on the natural desire to avoid trouble. If the prospect *really* doesn't want your product, there is no point in wasting any more time. Thank him for listening and try your luck elsewhere. But if you have reason to believe that he may change his mind, keep going.

If you have paid attention during your talk to the various signals sent out by the prospect, in the form of questions and objections, you should be well placed to assess his thinking. If you press too hard, too soon, he may withdraw into his shell. If you leave it too late, you may have missed your chance of converting that 'no' into a 'yes'. Some salesmen are blessed with a sixth sense which guides them towards the right strategy. But there are also various well-tried techniques which may help you to get the hoped-for result.

If you are selling to a corporation, the best time to strike is usually when a new executive has just arrived or when someone is leaving.

A new executive who is put into a decision-making role is anxious to make his mark. He will be receptive to ideas which will make him look good and his superiors will generally allow him to get on with it. Ask for an appointment – and don't hesitate to resurrect propositions which his predecessor may have rejected. He will have his own views on the merits of your product or service.

An executive who is about to leave no longer fears the consequences of a decision which may turn out to be wrong. The doubts which have prevented him from saying 'yes' in the past will cease to be important, and it may please him to make last-minute commitments. He may also want to please *you* because he hopes to do business with you in his new job.

The supersalesman always watches out for changes at the top of the corporate ladder and tries to make his move before his competitors have recognized their significance.

The trial close

The supersalesman does not necessarily wait until the end before he attempts to close. He may make his move at any time during the presentation. If he gets a positive response to what he is saying, he will seek to get the prospect to take a position on the benefits offered or on the suitability of the product. He may ask: 'Which colour do you prefer?' If the prospect says 'blue' he has indicated a willingness to buy. Or the salesman may say: 'Which delivery date would be best for you, the fifth or the tenth?' If the prospect replies: 'I need it by the fifth', he has virtually committed himself.

Often the prospect himself will provide an opening. He may ask: 'What are your credit terms and delivery dates?'

Or, perhaps, 'Will you install the new gas cooker?' Both questions may make it possible to close there and then. If he is not ready, you can easily say: 'Sorry, I didn't mean to push', and carry on with your presentation.

Assuming the sale

This ploy works best with timid people who find it hard to say 'yes' or 'no'. You simply take it for granted that your prospect has decided to buy and start writing up the order. The furniture salesman may say: 'Will somebody be at your home on Wednesday morning to receive the furniture?' The prospect hasn't actually said that he will definitely buy it, but he may be relieved that the decision has been made for him. 'Yes', he says, 'Wednesday morning will be fine.'

The inflation close

The prospect is tempted to buy, but can't quite bring himself to sign. Tell him that, with the cost of labour and raw materials going up, this may be his last chance to get your product at its present price. This gives him a justification for acting right away. A variation of this is used by real estate agents. 'At this price,' they say, 'the property won't be on the market long.'

The step-by-step technique

Many people find it difficult to make a major decision, but quite happily make a minor one. Ask the prospect a series of questions which he will find comparatively easy to answer. Do you agree that this machine would cut your costs and increase efficiency? Would you like it in black or green? Do you want to take advantage of our easy credit terms? Would you like to handle it on a monthly basis? Gradually, step by step, the rest of the decisions are made until the whole transaction is completed.

Give him the product

If you can't clinch the deal on the spot, offer to let him try out your product for a week or so. If you are selling, say, a computer to a first-time buyer he may find, at the end of the week, that he has grown so used to its benefits that he will gladly sign the order.

Car salesmen often find it worthwhile to let the prospect take the car home with him, calling a day or so later to ask if he is pleased with it. By then he will have shown it to his family – and the neighbours – and he will be eager to conclude the deal.

The planned pause

It often pays to remain silent after you have asked the closing question and leave the prospect to make the next move. Few people can stand silence for long and he will feel compelled to say *something*. He may agree to go ahead, or he may tell you that he will 'think it over'. If he is evasive, try to establish just what it is that he needs to think over. Is it the price? Is it the delivery date? This will give you another chance to identify the objection, deal with it, and attempt to close.

The supersalesman always tries to manoeuvre the prospect into a position where it is more reasonable to say 'yes' than 'no'. He knows that you can't win every time, but he has confidence in his product, is not afraid to ask for the order and doesn't give up at the first fence.

Why people say yes

They want to own what you have to offer.
They think it will benefit their company.
They fear that, if they don't buy now, they will have to pay
 more later on.
They can't resist the word 'new'.
They like spending money.

They like *you*.

They are not happy with their present suppliers and want to change.

They are in a hurry.

They think it will make them look good.

They want to take advantage of discounts.

They like making bold decisions.

They have heard that a rival has done well with your product/service and want to get into the act.

They don't have the courage to say 'no'.

They are greedy.

They feel insecure (a common reason for buying, say, insurance).

They are impressed by what you have done for others.

They need (or think they need) your product or services.

They are drunk/happy/in the right mood.

They are afraid that someone else will beat them to it.

Why people say no

They haven't been listening.

They only wanted to find out if you have any good ideas.

They are prejudiced against your product.

They don't like *you*.

They hate making decisions.

They don't have the authority to make decisions.

They haven't got the money.

They are afraid of the consequences of saying 'yes'.

They are tired/drunk/in the wrong mood.

They don't like change.

They haven't understood your presentation.

They are misers.

They are not convinced.

They know someone who will make a better offer.

They hope you will come back and improve your terms.

They don't like the colour/shape/feel of your product.

They are worried about your after-sales service.

Their wives/husbands won't let them say 'yes'.
They don't like your company.

ONCE YOU'VE SOLD, SHUT UP

Many salesmen don't know when to stop talking. They continue to sell *after* a commitment has been made – and, by doing so, run the risk of ruining the deal.

You will naturally want to get his order in writing, but if you force him to go over it all again he may have second thoughts.

You will be understandably eager to assure him that he has made the right decision, but if you praise him too effusively he may become suspicious.

You will obviously want to settle all the details, but if you raise new questions in his mind he may wonder what he has let himself in for.

You will naturally be happy that the prospect has said 'yes', but if you are *too* happy he may conclude that you have managed to get the better of him – that you are making too much out of the deal.

The supersalesman knows that, once you have made the sale, it pays to shut up. If the prospect indicates half-way through your presentation that he is willing to buy, don't plough on. More talk may simply trigger more objections. Don't say anything which could, just possibly, jeopardize his commitment. If you *must* keep talking, change the subject. Discuss the weather, golf, football, music – anything but the business you have just concluded.

Handling Objections

There are times in every salesman's life when he is sorely tempted to punch a prospect on the jaw.

Some people love to humiliate others, especially when they feel that there is little risk of retaliation. They rely heavily on the fact that the salesman wants the business and that he can't afford to lose his temper because it might cost him his job. So they make disparaging comments about his product or service, and object to just about everything he says. It makes them feel important.

You are unlikely to get anywhere with such obnoxious characters and the most sensible response, in most cases, is simply to stop the presentation. Say: 'I'm sorry you feel this way', put your notes back in the briefcase and move on to the next prospect.

But not all objections are based on a desire to hurt. More often than not, they are merely requests for more information. The prospect objects because he is not yet convinced: he can see problems and he wants to know what, if anything, can be done about them.

Some salesmen are so convinced of the merits of their product, and so determined to make a sale, that they resent *any* comment which seems to downgrade the proposition in any way. They take it personally. The supersalesman is more flexible. He knows how to distinguish between phoney and genuine objections, and he welcomes the latter because they show that the prospect is *interested* and because they give important clues to his real buying motives and needs. Some objections are simply tests of you and your knowledge of the product. Some are formalities. Not all can be overcome – there may be good reasons why the prospect does not wish to buy your product – but skilful handling can greatly improve your chances of success. The trick is to apply an appropriate technique.

Anticipate the objection

Most objections are not new and may even be predictable. They generally arise in some standard areas, such as price. If you have been selling your product or service for some time, you will be well aware of them and it is generally good strategy to build the answer into your presentation. Be sure to work it in early enough so that you avoid it coming up at all.

Ignore it

It sometimes pays to ignore the objection. Some people simply want to air their views (especially in front of colleagues) and are content when they have done so. They won't bring it up again. It is largely a matter of judgment. If you think the question is genuinely important to the buyer, deal with it there and then. Say: 'I am glad you raised that issue. Let me explain before we go on.'

Delay your response

If you can delay a resistance, you may be able to rob it of some of its strength. Again, this is a matter of judging how strongly he feels about it. If he thinks he is making a crucial point, tackle it head-on. But it often pays to say: 'I'm going to get to that in a few minutes, but let me talk about a few other points first.' He may have mellowed by the time you have finished your presentation.

Feed the objection back

Ask the prospect to elaborate his objection. He may, in the course of doing so, answer it himself or define it in such a way that it is easier for you to handle. If he says: 'But is it available in white?' throw a question back at him: 'Would you like it in white?' Whenever possible, get him to suggest a remedy. He may or may not have a workable solution, but once you have involved him in the process of finding one he is more likely to be on your side than against you.

Isolate the objection

Try to establish whether it is his principal objection – or even the only one. If he agrees that everything else is fine, he is backed into a corner. He has no other excuses. You merely have to deal with this one point to get the business.

Don't interrupt

Don't irritate the prospect by interrupting him when he is making an objection. Don't be impatient; hear him out, even if you think he is talking nonsense. Everyone likes to feel that he has a right to opinions of his own.

An insurance salesman had spent the best part of an hour trying to sell a company pension scheme and thought he was on the point of clinching the deal. But the prospect was one of those types who find it hard to make a decision. He scratched his head and said: 'I'll think it over.'

A lesser man might have assumed that it was a polite way of saying 'no'. But this was a supersalesman, so he smiled and said: *'Ah, in that case you qualify for our think-it-over plan.'*

He went on to explain that, while the prospect was doing his thinking, the insurance company would get on with all the paperwork.

A week later he telephoned the prospect, who told him that he was still thinking it over. 'What!' the salesman exclaimed. *'You mean you are thinking over our think-it-over plan?'*

He got the business.

Don't argue

Never tell a prospect that he is wrong (even if he is) or put him in a position where he has to defend himself or his point of view. If you do, he will fight you. He will lose sight of the merits of your product and will only be interested in resisting you. Remember that you are not there to win a debate; you are there to make a sale.

How Generous?

Bribery and Corruption

As every supersalesman knows, the borderline between a bribe and a genuine business gift – between corruption and the proper oiling of the wheels of commerce – is dangerously thin. In theory, almost everything worth having is illegal. In practice, the law generally turns a blind eye to gestures which are designed to promote goodwill. The problem is to decide how far one can go.

In countries like Britain and the United States, the rules were tightened up after the Lockheed scandal in the 1970s. The then chairman of Lockheed, you will recall, took the view that the end justifies the means. If 'payola' could secure the sales needed to keep the company going, it was cheap at the price. One had to take the world as one found it, not as one would like it to be.

He was not, of course, the first businessman to adopt this pragmatic approach, nor will he be the last. But it has become a risky game, especially if one is dealing with politicians and public servants. If the press gets to hear about it, there may be a lot of damaging publicity. Worse, both sides may (and sometimes do) end up in jail.

In Tokyo, a company director accused of corruption removed his trousers, cut his throat and slashed his wrists before jumping seven storeys to his death. It may strike you as a morbid example of Japanese thoroughness, but the suicide itself should not have caused any surprise. Bribery has become a particularly emotive issue in Japan, and oriental concern with loss of face increases the temptation to choose death as a way out.

Many companies nowadays play safe by forbidding employees to give or receive any gift which might conceivably be regarded as bribery. The fact remains, nevertheless, that in some countries corruption is a way of life. Bribes are not only accepted but expected. As *The Times* has said: 'In certain parts of the world the businessman is faced with a simple choice. Either he allows a bribe to be paid or he doesn't get the business.'

A former chairman of Shell once drew attention to another dilemma. He told a TV interviewer: 'I would like to ask some of the people who are becoming close to sanctimonious humbugs just what they would do if they had $200 million invested in a country and a politician with a death warrant in his pocket came along and said: "Give me ten million or else" – and the "or else" can take several forms. Would they pay it or would they refuse to pay? And if they did pay, would they say it was a bribe or would they not call it by its proper name – extortion?'

In some countries, bribery is known as 'dash'. There is also a practice called double-dash, which occurs when Mr A. pays a bribe to Mr B. on the basis that Mr B. will 'kick back' part of it to him. If either is caught, he may end up in jail. Unless, of course, he engages in treble-dash by buying his way out of trouble.

Lord Shawcross, who headed a commission set up by the International Chamber of Commerce to look at 'unethical practices', thought the answer was to ensure that those accepting the money were punished. But, he went on, an international agreement on a legal definition of bribery and corruption might be needed before any general law and penalties could be drawn up – and then there would remain the problem of enforcement.

Yes, there certainly would. That 'politician with a death warrant in his pocket' is not going to be eager to punish himself, and we can no longer send a gunboat to show such people the error of their ways. Many companies *do* pay bribes, but call them something else. There are all kinds of convenient euphemisms which make the practice sound better than it really is: 'commission', 'agent's fee', 'facility payment'. They agree with the former chairman of Lockheed: you can't afford to be too fussy.

You will, of course, have your own views on this. The temptation to take a chance is strong, but if you are worried about the ethics – and the law – you can refuse to do business with anyone, anywhere, who insists on a backhander. Someone else is sure to take over, but at least you won't have to follow the example of that Japanese director. Make sure, though, that the decision is taken by your board and that everyone fully understands why you have failed to win that coveted overseas contract. If they call you squeamish or naïve, you can always join another company.

The Art of Giving

The managing director was not amused. The sales director of a firm of suppliers had sent him what he no doubt thought was an hilarious gift: an Executive Problem Solver. It consisted of a small scaffold complete with a noose.

The sender had, alas, neglected to find out whether the managing director had a sense of humour. He didn't. As far as he was concerned, it was a childish gesture by a man who clearly could not be taken seriously in future.

The incident underlined a point which no one aspiring to be a supersalesman can afford to ignore: if you don't do your homework, gift-giving can do more harm than good. Some executives enjoy a little foolishness. Others find it irritating – even offensive. One has to know someone rather well before one can risk giving him, or her, one of the more dotty executive toys devised by the growing number of companies which specialize in such gimmicks.

Businessmen generally see gift-giving as a form of persuasion, and much of it is clumsy. The sales manager who dispatches half a dozen bottles of Scotch to his customers at Christmas, without bothering to find out whether they actually like Scotch, does not view it as a personal expression, a token of friendship. He seeks to create an obligation on the part of the recipient and, because his motives are so blatantly obvious, it often produces resentment rather than gratitude. People are offended by the implied suggestion that they can be bought so cheaply.

In many cases, the giver does not even take the trouble to send a letter with his gift: the store which delivers the bribes simply adds a typewritten card announcing the name of the sender. It is as crass as that other irritating practice – posting Christmas cards without bothering to sign them. If people can't make a little personal effort, they shouldn't spend any money at all.

Most of us are flattered by evidence that others have gone to some trouble to find out what will give pleasure. Thoughtfulness is appreciated all over the world.

Discreet enquiries will usually reveal the recipient's interests and hobbies. Books are generally welcomed. If he is keen on horses, get a book on horses. If he is mad about golf, give him the latest book on golf. It may be inadequate if you are trying to squeeze a multi-million contract out of someone who is used to lavish treatment, but never lose sight of the basic rule: whatever your motives, gifts should appear to be a personal expression of friendship and esteem.

Dealing with foreign business contacts requires extra care. You have to familiarize yourself with local customs as well as individual tastes. It is all too easy to make mistakes.

In some countries people will take offence if you arrive empty-handed; in others they will be no less offended if you turn up looking like one of those traders who bought Manhattan from the Indians for a few bottles of booze and a dozen strings of beads.

If you visit a French home for dinner, it is customary to send or bring flowers – but *not* Chrysanthemums, which represent mourning. In Germany, your hosts will be annoyed if you turn up with red roses – they are reserved for lovers. In Japan, considerable significance is attached to the way in which gifts are wrapped: ribbons have various meanings and a black-and-white wrapping combination is reserved for funerals. In the Arab world, it is bad form to bring a gift for a wife (or wives) and great care has to be taken in selecting items which depict animals or animal sculptures: many signify bad luck. If you are doing business in Latin America, do not give a knife (it implies cutting off a relationship) or a handkerchief (it's associated with tears).

Giving a home decoration is always risky. The recipient will feel obliged to display it. If he doesn't like it, he will be constantly reminded of your lack of consideration in selecting a gift. But elegant items made of silver are usually appreciated, and you are safe with presents for children, providing you choose something appropriate to their age group. Avoid logo gifts, unless they are unique.

The Japanese, who go to great lengths to establish a comfortable atmosphere for business, are probably the most gift-minded people in the world. But be careful not to create situations in which they may lose face. Don't surprise a Japanese businessman with a gift; he may be embarrassed by his not having one for you at the moment. Let him initiate the exchange and don't try to outdo him. Don't make a ceremony of a gift presentation; it should seem spontaneous and sincere but never a source of pride to the giver.

The Arabs, too, appreciate generosity. They have no respect for wealthy people who don't spend freely. As a result, they give much but expect to be treated equally well and have no shame about their belief in the utility of reciprocity. But don't admire an object openly: they may feel obliged to give it to you.

Some people prefer to wait until after a visit to send their tokens of appreciation. This has the twin merit of allowing you to travel lightly and discovering more about the other person's interests. You can always go to a local store or bookshop, or send some appropriate gift when you return home. It is very much a matter of individual judgment.

Choosing gifts

Yes	**No**
Flowers	Ash trays
Anything for the kids	A bottle of Scotch

Coffee table books
A subscription to *Punch*,
    the *New Yorker* or the
    National Geographic
Silver
Tickets to the latest hit
    play
Pocket TV
Banquet
Antique clocks
Golf clubs
Champagne swizzlesticks
Silk ties
Havana cigars
Concorde cuff-links
Gold pens
The Economist desk
    diary
A Rolls-Royce
Two first-class tickets
    to Barbados
A bottle of Dom Perignon
Regency wine coasters
Bonsai trees

Calculators
Pocket diaries
Fruit baskets
Papier-mâché boxes
Mobiles
T-shirts
Anything made of plastic
Joke stickers
Badges
Ball-point pens
A photograph of yourself –
    or, worse, your head
    office
Girlie calendars
Street signs
Cologne
Paintings (unless they are
    by Picasso or Van Gogh)
A subscription to *Playboy*
Company ties
Fruit salad jewellery
Western belt buckles

Jet
Lag

The Travelling
Salesman

Travel Talk

If your work involves frequent overseas travel, as mine does, you get used to envious comments from colleagues who feel chained to their office desks. 'Off again? Where to this time? Lucky devil. Can I carry your luggage?' They associate foreign travel with holidays and assume that every trip is a jolly romp. Some, of course, are just that. But there is nothing glamorous about going to Frankfurt, Zurich or Pittsburgh for the umpteenth time. You rush from one appointment to the next, sleep in an hotel room that is far less comfortable than your own home, drink too much and then hurry to an airport to catch a flight which is probably full and which, in the winter months, may be delayed by fog.

Inevitably, there are times when one wonders whether the journey was really necessary. Much of the world's business is now done by remote control. The telephone, the telex and, more recently, facsimile data transmission have, to a very great extent, taken the place of personal contact. The advantages are obvious – time is saved and often great expense as well.

But electronic communications will never replace the understanding and rapport engendered by meetings set up on a personal basis. You still have to sit down for detailed discussion and explanation (for example, in drawing up a contract or selling an idea). And face-to-face contact with new people, companies and factories can give you that instinctive feel for something, which is one of the salesman's biggest assets.

The supersalesman should aim to travel in comfort and style. He is doing an important job and I see no reason why he should be expected to exchange the sanitary, culinary and other comforts built into his private domain for miseries abroad. If your employers don't agree, ask them to send someone else.

Here are some comments on the basic aspects.

Expense accounts

The most important facility is, of course, an expense account. Travel is much more pleasant when someone else is paying: bills are less of a burden, being cheated is less painful and one is more likely to make friends. Expense accounts breed self-confidence, generosity and good humour. They are also good for trade. Anyone who doubts it need only look at Japan, where expenditure on entertaining alone exceeds the country's defence budget. No wonder the Japanese are so successful at selling their products.

In Europe and the United States, many executives do not have expense accounts as such: they have to take each bill along to the company's accountant, who exercises his right to be pedantic. Was it really necessary to have the Lafite '69? Wouldn't a later, and cheaper, vintage have done just as well? And how about this Duck Normand for $20, with truffles *and* Calvados? The supersalesman who has to chase business overseas should not put up with such nonsense. He may have to justify his expenses to the sales manager, or the managing director, but he should avoid accountants like the plague. They are not qualified to make such judgments. It pays, however, to take a few precautions. Keep a record of all your business appointments and as many receipts as possible. Make sure you get your sums right: don't give *anyone* a chance to query your claims.

Bless the jet

It's easy to take modern travel for granted. In Shakespeare's day it took as much as a week to get from London to Brighton and in the early nineteenth century the traveller to Italy still had to cross the Alps on foot, or be carried in a chair by porters. Today scheduled aircraft can get us *around the world* in fifty hours; Concorde regularly crosses the Atlantic in three-and-a-half hours. Yet few of us ever pause to reflect on our good fortune. It is extraordinary, when you think about it, that the only comment many people make at the end of a smooth transatlantic flight is that the steak was too tough or that the movie was one they had seen the week before. How blasé can you get?

The salesman has particular reason to be grateful for the modern jet – even if it is delayed from time to time. It has greatly widened his scope for doing business. Christopher Columbus would be amazed if he could see how easy it would be for him to reach the New World in the 1980s and Marco Polo would be equally astonished if he could see how many salesmen nowadays roam around China. Settled in their comfortable first-class sleeperseats, a glass of champagne by their side, they would be able to contemplate new conquests without any of the hassle involved in their own pioneering trips. Airlines are even experimenting with air-to-ground telephones.

The first-class cabin is, of course, the natural habitat for the supersalesman. Business class is very much second best: it's really an upgraded form of Economy which the airlines introduced in the 1970s in response to business travellers who objected to sitting among noisy tour groups. But it is the obvious choice if your company is too mean to buy you a first-class ticket; one of its merits is that you can book when you want, change or cancel without penalty, and even make stop-overs and change routings. Generally speaking, the better business classes are those with six abreast sitting downstairs or four abreast upstairs. They provide comfortable seats with at least thirty-eight inches of legroom, provide priority baggage handling and have separate lavatories. You also tend to get better treatment when things go wrong.

Many airlines have VIP clubs – such as the British Airways Executive Club – which allow access to airport lounges and provide a range of other benefits. Most charge an annual fee, but if you are a regular traveller the expenditure is well worthwhile.

What to take

Tourists generally take far too much luggage: they end up using only half, if that, of all the clothes and other things they pack. The salesman knows better. On short trips, the suit you are wearing is quite adequate – though it is generally advisable to add a raincoat. Shirts, socks and underwear can easily go into hand luggage, along with useful items like a small, battery-operated electric razor, a dictating machine, a pocket calculator, an adaptor which enables you to use electrical appliances anywhere in the world and a reliable quartz alarm clock. I also take a small set of jewellers screwdrivers, for use in dismantling recalcitrant electrical equipment, and a corkscrew. A pair of swimming trunks is a useful additional item, because many hotels nowadays have health centres complete with heated swimming pools, saunas and exercise areas. On Concorde and in first-class and business class they will allow you to bring a hanging bag for suits or dresses, so that you can walk off at the end of the flight without a long and tedious wait in the baggage hall.

If you are going on a long trip, a suitcase may be necessary. But I seldom take more than one, and I try to make it as light as possible. Porters are sometimes hard to find, and I have no desire to cart a lot of heavy luggage around airports.

Partners

There is, some businessmen insist, only one sure way of curing your wife of the notion that every trip is a mad romp. Take her with you. The result, alas, is not always so predictable.

Tactless hosts may suggest, in her presence, that you go to the *usual* nightclub. Female acquaintances may telephone, unaware that you are not alone. Hotel receptionists and restaurant managers may greet her like an old friend.

There is, moreover, a very real risk that you will end up having a good time. In short, the experiment may not only confirm her suspicions, but also make her determined to be part of *all* your business travel.

A lot, obviously, depends on your personal relationship – as well as on the elasticity of your budget. If your marriage has reached the point where you can't be together for more than twenty minutes without quarrelling, it's asking for trouble to take her with you. (The same, of course, applies if you are a female business traveller and your husband is keen to join you.) Tempers can, and do, rise when one is travelling and hotel rooms, inevitably, are more cramped than one's own home. Nor are you likely to have much fun if she hates meeting people, or spends all her time wondering whether the children, left in the care of grandparents or neighbours, are getting enough to eat. Your irritability will almost certainly be reflected in your behaviour towards associates.

I happen to enjoy my wife's company, and she loves to travel. So we frequently try to arrange joint trips. But we have a strict understanding that the work is shared: I take care of whatever business happens to be the purpose of the trip and she looks after the usual travel chores – packing, paying bills, tipping porters, telephoning airlines, making appointments, ordering breakfast, booking tables at restaurants and even typing letters when no secretary is available. Feminists may find this all wrong, but if *she* were going on a business trip, and decided to take me along, I would be quite content to see the roles reversed.

The arrangement has made me much more relaxed. We often extend our trips to include the weekend – and, in the process, see a lot of places we would otherwise miss. And, of course, we meet many more people. 'Your wife is with you?' a business contact will say. 'Wait a minute while I ring mine. Perhaps we can get together this evening.' It's not always a blessing: some couples can be an awful bore and, occasionally, good wine and brandy lead to indiscretions. 'In strictest confidence, old boy,' you say to your new friend, 'the firm's in a bit of trouble back home.' Or 'Don't pass this on, but we've got this great new idea – it'll make a fortune.' Wives, too, sometimes have an embarrassing urge to tell the truth and alcohol has an odd way of inducing rash promises. Next morning, sober again and conscious of how little you really know about your hosts, you wonder how you could have been so stupid. More often than not, however, such evenings develop into pleasant (and profitable) relationships.

There are, of course, countries where wives are expected to keep out of the way, and the visiting businessman should not feel slighted or rejected if he is not asked to dine *en famille*. Though the purdah has been lifted in many parts of Asia and North Africa, for example, the inbred seraglio tradition prevails psychologically. It is the rule, rather than the exception, for men to go out alone – even (or perhaps especially) after office hours. In Japan, too, your host is quite likely to suggest that you forget about the women. It's not merely that their proper place is thought to be at the kitchen sink; he will insist that you can't possibly enjoy yourselves if wives are present. So if your own wife has strong feminist feelings about this kind of attitude (and I, for one, don't blame her if she does) it would be wise to leave her at home. Supersalesmen can't afford to lecture people they are trying to do business with.

Mr and Mrs Smith

Some business travellers prefer to take *other* men's wives on business trips – or, perhaps, a nubile secretary. An American airline which offered free fares to accompanying wives some years ago sent out questionnaires asking them how they had enjoyed the experience. Most of the wives replied: 'What trip?' The husbands were understandably furious with the airline, and the offer was not repeated.

The basic rule must surely be the same as that for the office: if you must play, don't do it with a subordinate. People will usually find a way of telling your colleagues – and, perhaps worse, your wife – about the affair. You will be laughed at behind your back and superiors will express doubts about your judgment. Much better to choose someone who has no link of any kind with the company. A liaison with someone who works for a rival corporation may even be regarded as helpful; pillow talk can be a useful ally if one is interested in industrial espionage.

It isn't for me to make moral judgments, but there is no doubt that the world at large nowadays takes a much more lenient view of these things. Men don't hide their mistresses in back streets any more, and women are much more inclined to display their lovers. There *are* still countries where hotel clerks demand to see your passports and indignantly reject any attempt to check you into one room. (So book two.) And it is, as a rule, bad form to flaunt your companion at social occasions. It will embarrass people who have met your wife, and it will probably annoy your hostess – who visualizes her own husband doing the same when he travels abroad. Discretion pays.

Where to stay

'Hotel' is an extremely broad term, capable of covering everything from a dollar-a-night flophouse to the Ritz. The labels attached to the word can be annoyingly misleading. 'Luxury hotel' may simply mean that some of the suites have bathrooms. An 'hotel with atmosphere' can just mean an hotel with dirt. And 'Grand' frequently turns out to be a euphemism for old. Too many vulnerable establishments live on past reputations.

Modern hotels should be better, but all too often are not. Many are ugly concrete boxes which seem designed to handle packages rather than people. 'They are,' says Sir Hugh Casson, 'little more than filing cabinets in which personal and human contact are replaced by gadgets and anonymous facilities.'

One of my pet aversions is the big, brassy hotel which takes pride in its ability to attract mammoth conventions. Business travel is strenuous enough as it is without having to put up with gatherings of boisterous conventioneers. They have a way of taking over the place. You not only have to compete against them for room service, restaurant tables and the attention of receptionists and telephone operators, but they are liable to have parties in the room next to you late into the night or wake you up at 2 a.m. with loud conversation in the corridors. If you *have* to go to one of these jamborees – many are sales conventions – you might as well join in. But the individual salesman who is trying to get some rest after a busy working day would be well advised to choose a more tranquil base.

Some of the chain groups are, happily, aware that size can be a handicap as well as an asset and have set up separate luxury wings of floors in their hotels. I recommend that you ask to be booked into these oases. You don't have to be a snob to appreciate exclusiveness.

I am very fond, myself, of small, clubby establishments where the accent is on personal service. You will find many of these in my guide, *The World's Best Business Hotels*, which covers more than 500 hotels in 80 countries and offers independent assessments.

What most of us really need is a good hotel, in a central location, which has the kind of facilities which make it possible to do business with the minimum of hassle. These include direct-dial telephones, an efficient telex service and a reliable message-relaying system. I also appreciate a desk in the room, individual temperature control, a direct dial telephone, a well-stocked mini-bar, tea and coffee making facilities, and a colour TV with video programmes in a language that I can understand. A good restaurant is a bonus; so is a disco, providing you aren't forced to listen to the music (because they haven't bothered with sound-

---

Different cultures pose all kinds of hazards for the travelling salesman.

In Thailand, for example, it is considered rude to point your feet at anyone: if you sit with your legs crossed, make sure your toes are pointed to the floor.

In the Arab world it is considered bad manners to start talking about business the moment you meet. Allow time for small talk and never raise the subject of business first: let the prospect do it. (Sometimes he doesn't get around to it at all, which is maddening. Ask, before you leave, if you can come and see him on another day.)

Japanese businessmen are exasperatingly fond of ambiguity and vagueness. Don't offend them by being too direct and insisting on clarity and precision.

Germans tend to be formal in their relations and expect the same behaviour from you. Don't address them by their first name until you have got to know them really well and have been given permission to do so.

The Russians are very strict with foreigners who are caught making deals (especially foreign currency transactions) on the black market. You never know who you are doing business with; don't take chances.

It always pays to check up on these things before visiting a country for the first time. There is no excuse for stumbling into a situation which could wreck the whole trip. Follow the local customs, don't talk about politics (and, in Arab countries, about subjects like the status of their women), go easy on the jokes and try to stay reasonably sober, if you can.

---

proofing) when all you want is a good night's sleep. If you know such an hotel, make it your home from home – if your expense account can stand it. There is a lot to be said for being treated like a friend and not just another computer number.

How to handle jet lag

Not even the most relentless workaholic is likely to schedule a meeting for the middle of the night. Yet this is what a salesman does by going to a meeting in, say, Paris or London at 9 a.m. after flying all night from New York, a time when the traveller's biological clock says it is three or four in the morning – F. Scott Fitzgerald's 'dark night of the soul'.

Everyone knows the symptoms of jet lag – buzzy head, strained eyes, general fatigue and disorientation. Even for high-flying achievers this can make for a distinctly subsonic performance and bizarre business decisions, especially hazardous when the people around you are at their sharpest. It doesn't last very long – the body clock soon adjusts itself – but may be long enough to louse up a promising deal.

Doctors generally advise a twenty-four-hour rest whenever there has been a long flight with a five-hour time change. But this is easier said than done: the temptation to rush off to appointments is difficult to resist. Another approach, which I favour, is to stay on your home schedule and ignore what is going on around you. But the best way to handle jet lag is to get a good night's rest before you leave, sleep as much as possible on the plane (even if it means taking short-acting tablets), eat sparingly and drink plenty of fluids (but go easy on the booze).

Despite some contradictory evidence from scientific studies, most people say they get more jet lag flying east than west. It seems that people have less trouble coping with a subjectively long day than a short night. If possible, travel in the daytime and on really long journeys stop at least once along the way. I once travelled to Australia in one go, and it took me a week to get back to normal. The second time, I stopped for a couple of days in Bangkok and not only had a good time but arrived in a much happier frame of mind. And, of course, the airline made no extra charge.

Perhaps the most promising news on jet lag is the work on melatonin by the University of Surrey. Melatonin is a sleep-inducing hormone secreted by the pineal gland at the front of the brain. Melatonin levels are higher at night than during the day, which has led researchers to believe that it may be a master synchronizer of various biological rhythms. According to them, if you administer melatonin during the day you can resynchronize the biological clock by deceiving the body into thinking that it is night. A product based on this discovery is being developed; it should be a winner.

EXCUSES YOU SHOULD NEVER HAVE TO USE

I didn't know you were in a hurry for it.
That's not my department.
No one told me to go ahead.
I'm waiting for approval.
That's the way we have always done it.
I forgot.
My secretary lost the order.
I'm so busy, I just haven't been able to get around to it.
That's his job, not mine.
The post is so unreliable.
I needed more information, but couldn't get hold of you.
Tom/Dick/Harry said he would handle it.
I thought I told you.
We lost your address.
It isn't the 14th already, is it?

How to Make the Most of Advertising

Awesome! Brilliant! Fabulous!

Advertising people love to use superlatives, and their clients are naturally pleased when they hear them applied to their own products – or, better still, themselves. 'Mr Jones, your vision of the company's future is *awesome*. Your management team is *brilliant* and your new soap/car/watch/perfume/cheese/computer is *fabulous*.'

The chief aim of this exaggerated flattery is to win new accounts and protect the ones they already have. Competition is fierce – so much so that one New York agency man asked by Gallup why he wouldn't want his son to go into advertising explained: 'Because he might steal my accounts.'

This, of course, is very pleasant for marketing and sales managers who have to decide which agency deserves their company's business. For once the roles are reversed: the supersalesman is the prospect.

Advertising agencies have trendy offices, with plush carpets, long-legged blonde secretaries and lots of people with the word 'director' in their title. If your account is substantial – i.e. if you spend a lot of money on advertising – the chief executive will buy you expensive lunches and invite you to Ascot. Some prospects manage to eat well for months, without spending any of the company's money, by simply encouraging a number of agencies to think that they might, just might, get their business.

It is, of course, dumb to choose an agency on the basis of its flattery and generosity. What *really* counts is the answer to the question: will its efforts help to sell your product? Look at the advertisements they already do for other clients. How good is it? Does it sell? Some of the most effective campaigns in recent years have *shunned* superlatives. Avis, for example, did remarkably well with its slogan: 'When you're only No. 2, you try harder.' And Volkswagen had a tremendous hit in America with its simple message: 'Think Small.'

Advertising, we are told, 'is the equivalent in print of salesmen knocking on doors and selling face-to-face'. But much of the advertising one sees today – on TV as well as in print – is very far from having a doorstep manner. Some is deliberately snobbish and some is entertainingly flippant. Neither would work well on the doorstep. Gimmicks abound. As Arnold Gingrich, former publisher of *Esquire*, has put it: 'You have a hard time today to find an ad that isn't so busy being different it forgets to be an ad. Par for the course is an eye patch on one eye and a monocle on the other, topped by a beret and bordered by a bear, riding backwards on a zebra, wearing tails with red shoes and using a violin for a croquet mallet. When all around you are being too, too clever, then it's smart to be plain.'

If advertising didn't sell, companies would hardly spend such vast sums on it. But you certainly cannot take it for granted that *every* campaign will produce the hoped-for results. The wrong advertisement can actually *reduce* the sales of a product or service. And there is nothing much an agency can do about a product that is clearly inferior to its rivals. It may succeed in boosting sales for a brief time, but the consumer won't buy it again, which is a waste of everybody's money.

A good agency will insist on being fully briefed. It will want as much information as possible about your company's finances and production, the brands, the marketplace, the consumer, previous advertising and so on. Some companies take more trouble over this than others. When Guinness decided that it needed a new campaign the management prepared a 100-page document, topped by a 10-page summary of the problem. Its senior executives went to see each of the short-listed candidates and gave them a presentation on the marketplace, the brand and how consumers use and understand the brand. They even got down to the tone and style of the advertising by saying, for example, that they wanted it to be 'witty but not too smart' and 'generally believed but not flippant'.

Many other managements settle for a chat in which they outline what they want to achieve and then step back and leave it to the agency to say how it should be done. A lot of agencies prefer this relatively casual approach, but it obviously helps to be familiar with every aspect of a client's business.

Who's who

The chief executive will probably bring along his creative director, who will listen to your brief and tell you what the agency can do for you. Once the account has been won, the big men will drop out of the picture – though they will probably continue to buy you lunch from time to time, to make sure that you won't run off to another agency. Other people will do the actual work. Only about 10 per cent of an agency's staff are involved in the actual process of producing advertisements. Here are the people who really count.

The account executive

The account executive is the man – or woman – who is responsible for day-to-day contact with the client. He or she is the person who has to listen patiently to your suggestions and complaints, and who will do his best to extract the best possible work from the agency's other departments – a task which often leads to monumental rows. (You don't, of course, get to hear about them.) Make sure that he is genuinely interested in your product, keep him well

WHAT THEY SAY	WHAT THEY MEAN
This is an exciting product.	I want your account.
We will do some research.	We can't believe you haven't done any yourself; how backward can you be?
Advertising is the most effective and efficient way to sell to the customer.	We can't prove it works, but you can hardly expect us to say so.
We have decided not to pitch for this account.	We are not going to risk being turned down.
This is a tremendous challenge.	We doubt if anyone will want to buy this product, but we'll have a go.
We think humour would be inappropriate for this campaign.	It's going to be hard enough to get anyone to take the product seriously as it is.
What an interesting idea.	A terrible idea, but it pays to keep the client happy.
We will look at it again.	There is nothing wrong with this ad, but we don't want to lose the account.
How much do you want to spend?	Are we going to make any money out of this?

briefed and try to cultivate his friendship. It generally turns out to be well worthwhile.

The copywriter

The copywriter works behind the scenes and you may never get to meet him. If and when you do, he may turn out to be a rather scruffy and temperamental individual – one reason why his superiors prefer to keep him away from clients. But from your point of view, he is the most important person in the agency, because he has to think up ideas for advertising campaigns and write the words. (The text is always known as 'copy'.) Good copywriters also have the ability to think visually, which is especially important if you are doing a TV commercial.

The art director

The art director is responsible for the graphic elements in advertisements – layout, photography and typography. He is the person who will constantly remind the copywriter (if he should need reminding) that 'a picture is worth a thousand words'. Many art directors have turned themselves into television producers and they often go on to become creative directors – the people responsible for all the creative work – with a seat on the Board.

Dos and don'ts

DO look for a big idea. Your advertisement has to compete with a multitude of others, and it takes a big idea to attract the attention of the consumers. It doesn't have to be complex: simple but dramatic concepts are often the best. One of the most famous – and most successful – ads of all time was the 'Guinness for Strength' poster which showed a man carrying a huge girder on his head. The concept was so outrageous that it caught the public's imagination. People in pubs even took to asking for a girder.

DO make sure that the advertisement is relevant to your

product. Some agencies seem more interested in impressing each other – and winning awards – than in selling what the client has to offer. Their ads may be eye-catching, but don't necessarily achieve the results **you** want.

Many creative people think it's smart to stick a nude in ads for anything, including heavy machinery. But sexual appeals are often counter-productive in the sense that, unless they are directly relevant to the product advertised, they can distract attention from it. The same is true of celebrities: people tend to remember the celebrity while forgetting the product.

DO decide what 'image' you want for your brand. Products, like people, have personalities, and they can make or break them in the marketplace. Every advertisement should be thought of as a contribution to the brand image. If it works, stay with it until it stops selling. Marlboro has used its highly successful 'cowboy' theme for more than twenty-five years.

DON'T try to write the ad yourself. Some marketing and sales people can't keep their hands off advertisements; they not only insist on giving explicit instructions – 'the logo must be blue' – but also mess around with the actual copy. Sometimes a committee gets to work on an ad and completely ruins it. There is no point in hiring an agency if you won't allow it to do the job.

DON'T haggle over the agency's compensation. The cheapest won't necessarily be the best – and you want the best. Remember that you are not buying supplies but creative talent. Ask the agency what it charges and, if you are satisfied that it can do the job better than its competitors, pay the price. Cost alone should never be the deciding factor.

DON'T keep changing agencies. Some companies believe in management by fear. They like to keep everyone, including the advertising agency, in a perpetual state of anxiety. The assumption is that, by doing so, they can ensure that everyone will do his best. This is a questionable premise, to say the least. Frightened people are much more likely to play safe by simply agreeing with everything the client says, even if their professional judgment tells them that he is talking nonsense. Big agencies will often resign an account rather than put up with this kind of thing, and I don't blame them. You have a better chance of getting good results if the relationship is a happy one. If you don't like what your agency is doing, or if its efforts fail to produce the expected increase in sales, by all means say so. Give the

Many companies nowadays spend huge sums on promoting their 'corporate image' instead of their products. For some it's vanity, a purely cosmetic change, the appeasement of a boardroom whim. But for many more it has a serious purpose.

Corporate advertising can make a good impression on the investment community and often has an influence on legislation. It also boosts the morale of employees and helps to improve the public's perception of the company: research shows that people who know a company well are five times more likely to have a favourable opinion of it.

In some cases, corporate advertising campaigns are designed to indicate a real change of direction. Many companies grow away from their original product and their name becomes inappropriate. A new identity can reduce the risk of misunderstanding. Mergers are another classic reason for name and style changes. They allow the management to claim that a genuine merging of talents and not just a take-over has taken place.

If you get involved in a corporate campaign, do your best to avoid pomposity and blatantly self-serving statements. If you are advertising in the national press, or on television, keep it simple. Don't ask the chairman or the chief executive to appear in his own commercials; it is nearly always a bad idea.

creative people an opportunity to come up with something better. If they can't, then (and only then) change your agency.

Market Research

Kindly answer these questions. Do you like this book? If not, why not? What sort of book would you like to have bought instead? Then why on earth didn't you? What do you think of market research? Do you: a) find it a waste of time; b) think it's the only way to sell; c) don't know what it's all about?

Market research is booming because it is a convenient way of 'confirming' your own hunches. At one time, people were content to put a product on the market and wait to see what happened. If it sold, they made more. If it didn't, they stopped production. Today the emphasis is on 'scientific decision-making based on the collection and evaluation of appropriate facts'.

A whole new industry has been built on this need for assurance that one is doing the right thing. The public is subject to an increasingly fierce bombardment by questionnaire. It irritates the busy, cheers the lonely and flatters the insignificant. Who will you vote for? What beer do you like best? Will you buy this new product? The answers are reduced to numerical form, cross-analysed by standard categories such as the age, sex and social class of each person interviewed, and served as a tasty-looking dish.

Market research started with the intention of finding out who bought a particular product and why. It has since advanced to the point where many products are designed to fit in with the researcher's findings. In theory, this avoids waste in producing things that won't sell, makes it possible to direct sales campaigns at a carefully targeted group of consumers. In practice, market research often leads

companies up the garden path. It is a pseudo-science and the people who make it all sound so impressive, with the help of fancy jargon and tomes of statistics, are as fallible as everyone else. Just look at the opinion polls which so worry the politicians – and which so often get it wrong.

Every supersalesman sooner or later has to face the question of what to do about this trendy type of sorcery. The answer is simple: use it, but treat it with caution.

Research is supposed to tell you not only what people are buying, or what they are likely to buy, but also what kind of packaging will sell best and how consumers rate a new product compared with its rivals.

The problem, though, is that the results may turn out to be unreliable. Sometimes too few people are consulted: it is not uncommon for market surveys, intended to be the basis for 'scientific decision-making', to be based on replies from fewer than thirty people. And there is no guarantee that consumers will tell the truth. Some simply tell the interviewer what they think he or she wants to hear. Others, in a hurry to get away from the interviewer, reply without giving the matter any serious thought. Some even amuse themselves by deliberately giving phoney answers.

The market researchers in your company (if you have them) will no doubt counter that, despite these handicaps, their methods work. Remind them of the Edsel. The Ford Motor Company spent a fortune on market studies prior to launching that disastrous model. And if they dismiss that as a fluke, tell them about Coca Cola's unhappy experience in 1985. The company, worried because it was losing market share to Pepsi, introduced a 'new Coke' early in the year after its researchers had conducted 200,000 taste tests in which 55 per cent of those surveyed had chosen the new product. The theory of random sampling holds that 55 per cent is adequate proof that people prefer the new product, all other things being equal. But all other things were not equal. Marketplace reaction to the withdrawal of the original formula was most emphatically negative, and ten weeks later the president solemnly announced the return of the old Coca Cola.

Research is no substitute for judgment.

There are times when market research can be very helpful, even if you don't believe in it. Your lack of faith is not important; what matters is that *others* are likely to treat research with respect.

It can support your case

If you have made up your mind to follow a certain course, but have not yet succeeded in persuading your colleagues to go along, commission some market research. Use an outside firm and let it be known what kind of result you expect; you can usually obtain a favourable interpretation of the data, because the firm will want to go on earning handsome fees. Use the data to defeat the doubters. If, by some chance, the research should fail to support you, file the report, sack the researchers and carry on arguing.

It can be used to kill ideas

If you think that someone else's project is terrible, get the market researchers to produce a study which casts doubt on the whole exercise. Be sure to include plenty of statistics. People are absurdly impressed by figures, even though everyone knows that they can be made to dance to any tune you want to play.

It can be used as a scapegoat

If you launch a sales campaign on the basis of your hunches, it may go wrong and you will get the blame. If you use market research and the campaign goes wrong, you have someone else to blame.

What they say	**What it means**
This is raw data.	We have an awful lot of stuff, but we haven't worked out what it means. (Have nothing to do with it; insist on a succinct report that indicates the results of the research.)
We believe in scientific decision-making.	We believe in finding some statistical basis for the decisions you want to make – and charging you a handsome fee.
We must go into the field.	We must get out of the office and talk to customers.
We recommend in-depth interviews.	We are going to give Joe's mother-in-law a chance to talk for hours.
We suggest concept testing.	We don't think much of your idea, but we will try to find out how other people feel about it before you go ahead and make a fool of yourself.
On the one hand, on the other hand.	We are not sure what to make of the results, so we have decided to waffle. (Tell them they are paid to come up with firm conclusions.)
Broken down by age and sex.	Not a description of the chairman; simply a way of analysing answers.

This is based on blind testing.

The products tested have not been identified by their brand because it might influence comparisons and reflect the brand image rather than 'pure' product characteristics.

Studies have shown that the degree of correlation between socio-economic characteristics and consumption is quite small and the practice of using demographics as a basis for deriving media strategies can be challenged.

This research is useless.

Public Relations

Public Relations

Public relations is widely regarded as a form of sales-manship, especially by those who foot the bill. The people who call themselves 'PR executives' prefer a more pretentious definition. 'Public relations,' they will tell you, 'means developing and maintaining understanding between an organization and its public.' The fact is, nevertheless, that most of it involves selling of some kind or another. PR people are employed to ensure that an organization is well known and well thought of – by the public, by the industry, by the financial world, by politicians and by its own workers. They sell ideas and images as well as services and products.

Sometimes PR actually gets in the way of understanding. Part of the job of the PR executive, as most employers see it, is to act as a first line of defence when things go wrong. On those occasions he is expected to lie with equanimity – or at least to refrain from telling the truth, which often amounts to much the same thing.

The supersalesman should be thoroughly familiar with the various methods used in public relations. He should certainly know what it can and cannot do.

A common assumption is that one can get free editorial publicity for just about anything a company wants to promote. There are, to be sure, trade publications which will usually oblige, especially if you promise to bribe them by placing some advertising, but important newspapers and magazines are much more discriminating. A story must have genuine news value, and a good journalist will want to write it in his own way.

Here are some of the most common ways of 'placing' a story.

The press release

Information in written form, sent to the press in the hope of getting an editorial mention. Many press releases are advertisements masquerading as news stories; they please the company's executives, who are easily persuaded that something useful has been done – even if it doesn't result in a single column inch of actual coverage. Don't be misled: make sure your company has a 'cuttings' service and insist on having access to it.

A good press release is short and to the point. Stimulate interest by giving the hard news in the first paragraph, and avoid jargon and long-winded elaboration. Make sure that it reaches the right person. Ideally, separate versions should be sent to each publication; if this is impossible, at least try to remember that the trade press tends to see things differently from the national press. Give your name and telephone number, so that journalists can ask for more information. If they don't call you, call *them* and ask if they want to know more. It will at least ensure that they actually *read* what you have sent them. Some PR people make doubly sure by wrapping their press release around, say, a half bottle of champagne: it doesn't guarantee coverage, but it does get attention.

The press kit

A more elaborate version of the press release which generally includes pictures and background information on the organization. It can be useful if you are trying to sell an interesting new product or service, and have invited journalists to a press conference or factory tour.

The press conference

Press conferences are held for a variety of reasons: to

launch a new product; to make an important policy state-ment; to announce the annual results; to explain a certain course of action. The main advantage is that you can sell in person and establish useful contacts. The pitfall, though, is that journalists can ask awkward questions and use your answers to write a story which is quite different from the one you had in mind. The press is always on the look-out for an angle – preferably one with an element of controversy – and an unguarded remark can have embarrassing conse-quences. Ask your PR people to tell you in advance what kind of questions are likely to be asked and watch what you say. Take extra care if you have invited everyone to stay for a drink: skilled reporters often get their best stories when the formal proceedings are over.

The press visit

It is always a good idea (unless, of course, you have something to hide) to invite the press along to see your new factory, process, or whatever. It may not result in immediate publicity, but there are often considerable long-term bene-fits. You will have made new friends, who can be contacted directly when you have some news, and they will be more inclined to give you a favourable editorial mention if they have actually seen what you do.

Keep the numbers small (important journalists should be invited individually) and lay on a good lunch. If you have a new consumer product, make sure your visitors get a sample to take home. If you are selling a service, offer to let them try it.

Interviews

Interviews can be very useful, and you don't have to wait to be asked. They can be set up. But remember a few basic points:

    – Your colleagues are liable to get jealous. Chairmen and/or chief executives are particularly inclined to complain if someone else attempts to hog the limelight, even if it's good for business. Don't speak for an organization unless you have clearance from the top.

– Make some enquiries, beforehand, about the person who will be doing the interview. Some people are fair; others think it's smart to be bitchy. Never make the mistake of automatically assuming that the interviewer will be eager to do you a favour.

– If you are interviewed for a newspaper or a magazine, provide as much background information as you can. It is astonishing how often journalists manage to get even the most basic facts wrong; you can reduce the risk by giving them a written summary. Speak *slowly*: if they haven't clearly understood what you have said, they are liable to be quite shameless about making up quotes, which can be embarrassing. Be enthusiastic, but not bombastic. Ask if you can see the finished article before publication so that you can check it for facts. They will probably say no, but it doesn't hurt to try.

– If you are invited to appear on radio or TV, try to ensure that it's a 'live' interview. Tapes are invariably edited – often heavily – and the result can be counter-productive. Keep your answers short and avoid jargon. By all means mention your product, but remember that most radio and TV people get mad if you overdo the plugging.

The lunch

PR executives love to take people to lunch – indeed, some appear to do little else. The assumption is that good food and wine will produce favourable publicity, or at least put a stop to criticism. It sometimes works, but a great many of these lunches are an expensive waste of time. They can also be dangerous, because garrulous PR types, eager to impress their guests, may give away more than they should.

Some organizations have regular 'media lunches', which often turn into an informal press conference. Half a dozen journalists are invited to meet top executives and are encouraged to ask questions. It *can* create a lot of goodwill, but the host should always make it quite clear whether the conversation is on or off the record.

Public Crisis

The true test of PR people is how they handle a crisis.

Faced with bad news, the natural reaction of most top executives is to suppress it. 'You don't wash your dirty linen in public,' they insist.

If there is a leak, the PR people may be asked to issue a denial or to say 'No comment'; this can be taken to mean the story is true.

The aim is to protect the company's reputation, but it frequently has the opposite effect. As Richard Nixon found, the press has ways of getting at the truth and can be disconcertingly persistent. A company which is caught lying inevitably harms its image – which is bad salesmanship, not to mention the possible legal implications.

It is usually more sensible, if there is a leak, to admit that something has gone wrong and *that you have taken instant action to put it right.* It will make you, and your organization, look reassuringly positive.

Then there is the matter of press criticism. Let us assume that you have launched a new product and an attacking article is printed. You may think the comments unfair, and will be tempted to launch a counter-offensive.

You can get your lawyers to write a threatening letter and *perhaps* the paper will publish a retraction. But you won't be forgiven – the journalist concerned, and his colleagues, will never write another kind word about you or your company and will, in all probability, use every opportunity to have a go at you.

You can also write to the editor, complaining in the

strongest possible terms about the article and threatening to cancel all advertising unless his paper prints an immediate apology. *Don't do it.* Nothing irritates an editor more than the threat of economic pressure: the chances are that he will not only repeat the criticism in the next day's paper but also accuse you of trying to stifle the unbiased reporting of his journalists. Before you know it, papers will have taken up the story and your product will suffer still further damage.

The best course is to respond more in sorrow than in anger. Call the journalist and offer to supply more information which may help him to write another, more favourable, story. If that doesn't work, write a letter for publication which gives your side of the argument. Don't belittle the journalistic ability and integrity of the person who wrote the original article: stick to the facts and let the reader judge who is right.

What they say	**What it means**
I'm not a salesman.	I *am*, but I resent being taken for one – it's so undignified.
I'll do my best.	I don't think anyone will be interested in this story, but I want to get you off my back, so I'll write a press release.
Let's run a competition.	I can't think of anything new, so we might as well try an old idea.
He is a very good friend of mine.	I met him once, at a cocktail party.
No comment.	The things I could tell you! But I'm not going to risk my job by getting involved in this one.

We'll run this story in the house journal.	No one else will print it.
We'll need a quote from the chairman.	The chairman likes to see his name in the papers.
We must have a launch party.	It won't do much good, but I *love* parties.
I've arranged for you to be interviewed for radio.	The television people said no, but I found a small local radio station which will put you on after midnight.
I don't think a press conference would be a good idea.	This story is so trivial that no one would bother to turn up.
Let's take the editor out to lunch.	I want to try that new place – I hear they have marvellous *foie gras* and *filet mignon de porc normande* – but the prices are outrageous. I'll provide the excuse; you pay the bill.
Hallo, old boy.	I wish I could remember your name.
I am concerned about our image abroad.	I need a holiday in the sun and I want the company to pay.
I'll mention it to the chief executive.	I'm not taking any orders from *you*.

Public relations does not *necessarily* involve contact with the media – indeed, much of it is kept well away from the eyes of prying journalists.

Political PR aims to influence legislators and bureaucrats, who nowadays have such a big say in what an organization can or cannot do. It may mean selling an idea or project which requires official approval, or it may involve trying to stop action which is perceived to be against the organization's interest.

Financial PR means being nice to shareholders, especially financial institutions. The aim is to persuade them to think well enough of your company to put up more funds, when required, and to take your side if there is trouble – if, for example, there is an unwelcome take-over bid.

Community PR tries to enhance your company's standing in the area – or areas – in which it operates. It makes it easier to get planning permission if you want to put up a new factory.

Internal PR takes in everything to do with employees – keeping them informed, preventing strikes and so on.

Corporate PR is concerned with selling an organization's image rather than its products or services. It involves such things as print, packaging, advertising and letter-headings. It *should* also involve training receptionists and telephone operators, who between them can do more to wreck your image than anyone else.

The Rewards of
Success

Now the Good News

The rewards of success in selling are pleasant to contemplate – more income, a bigger expense account, promotion, travel to exotic places, and even the opportunity to start your own business. You no longer have to dream about these things; they are within reach. The income of many supersalesmen is well into six figures. Not surprisingly, they are much envied by less fortunate colleagues.

Every successful salesman naturally wants to keep as much of his income as possible. But not everybody shares his ambition. The Inland Revenue certainly doesn't. The top tax rates have been reduced from the ridiculous levels which existed under the last Labour Government, but the taxman still takes a considerable slice.

The search for tax efficient ways has spawned some of the most complex weaves of fringe benefits, from the ubiquitous company car through family medical schemes, subsidized school fees, concessionary home loans, incentive travel and even executive clothing allowances. The Inland Revenue keeps a wary eye on all of them, but it is obviously worth finding out what your employers offer their top people and making sure that you get your share of it.

The incentive game

Motivating high fliers in sales by offering rewards other than cash has become big business: there are, nowadays, numerous firms which specialize in this field. They argue that, once a salesman has reached his 'comfort level', cash incentives begin to lose their effect because people are no longer prepared to work any harder simply to earn more highly taxed money. It is, they maintain, 'the point at which an alternative method of remuneration is necessary if the motivational momentum is to be sustained'. This may strike you as a somewhat dubious proposition – cash is still very important to most of us – but there is no doubt that the incentive game has become very popular.

One company specializes in what it calls 'bonus bonds', which are retail vouchers that can be spent in over 8,500 shops, hotels and travel agencies in the UK. Others offer catalogues of merchandise, the items in which can be earned on a points basis. Everything, from decanters to food mixers and tape recorders, is available as a 'prize' for those who have achieved something – preferably something beyond the call of duty. 'The salesman takes it home,' says a leading specialist, 'and someone will say to him: "That's a nice tape-recorder, Philip. Where did you get it?" That gives him a chance to explain how he won it.'

But the most popular incentive of all is travel. Some £50 million a year is spent by British business alone; in America, the figure is put at a staggering $2 billion. The reasons for this are not difficult to fathom. Travel of some sort is the ultimate dream of most people. It is also something which bears repetition – someone who has been to Barbados may be happy, and even eager, to go again if offered the chance, for free, while someone who already has a tape-recorder or video machine might be less enthusiastic about being given another one. Travel has a broad family appeal, so employees and business contacts who are offered such an incentive are able to share the anticipation – and the trip – with their wives and, sometimes, their children.

The heaviest users of this type of incentive both in Europe and North America tend to be the insurance and motor industries. Insurers use it to motivate salesmen and brokers; car manufacturers find it an effective method of rewarding dealers.

The problem for the participants is that the Inland Revenue may want to tax the benefit. The way around this, usually, is to combine business with pleasure – to argue that you are using the trip to pursue new sales opportunities. But this is obviously more difficult to justify if you are taking your family. The best way to ensure that the taxman will leave you alone is to go as part of a group and claim that the primary purpose is to discuss business away from the normal environment. The Inland Revenue is rarely in a position to check that you have, indeed, spent most of your time talking about work. Not surprisingly, group travel is the fastest-growing sector of the market.

How much money?

It may well be, of course, that you still have quite a way to go before you reach your 'comfort level'. Terms like these tend to mean different things to different people. For some, comfort is a cosy suburban home, nice furniture and a family car. For others, it means a country estate, a Rolls-Royce, a yacht and a house in the South of France. I know rich businessmen who insist that they need £100,000 'just to survive'.

Many salesmen over-reach themselves financially because they are confident that they will be able to boost their earnings – somehow. Being in debt, they maintain, is a spur to greater effort. Considering that they spend so much of their time persuading *others* that there is nothing wrong with borrowing, it would be surprising if they felt otherwise. But there are bound to be anxious moments. The hoped-for bonuses may fail to arrive; commissions may fall short of expectations; the company they work for may go out of business.

Employers generally set targets and reward those who exceed them. The supersalesman shouldn't find it hard to do so, providing the targets are realistic, but even he occasionally has a rough patch. Deals may turn sour through no fault of his own. Like everyone else, he also has to decide whether the pursuit of cash should outweigh all the other factors – job satisfaction, a good environment, a happy home life. Some companies pay very well but are terrible to work for.

His great advantage, compared to most of his colleagues, is that he is used to handling difficult negotiations. He knows how to see things from the other man's point of view (in this case, the employer) and he is quite capable of assessing what he is worth to him. He also knows that many other companies would probably be glad to acquire his services. This gives him considerable bargaining strength, and no one can blame him for making the most of it.

It is, however, important to be as realistic about this as about targets – or anything else. Many people over-estimate their worth. Some get their timing wrong; they push too hard, too soon. And some play the 'I-may-leave-card' without first finding out whether others really need their services as badly as they like to believe. We all know how readily some sales managers make promises – 'If you ever decide to leave, we'd be happy to have you' – and how often they back-pedal when you go to see them *after* you have left. The unemployed salesman has lost much of his bargaining power.

Some companies try to tie their best people down by offering them a service contract. In a volatile business like selling, there is obviously much to be said for accepting it. If things go wrong, you are well placed to demand generous compensation. But service contracts also restrict your room for manoeuvre. If an attractive offer comes along, you may not be in a position to accept it. Most employers will release people who are eager to move, because an unhappy salesman is no good to anyone, but you can't *count* on it. They can just as easily insist that you serve the full term; the contract which seemed so reassuring when you signed it may come to look more like a prison sentence.

The profit motive is as important to individuals as it is to companies. If you are not keen to make money, you shouldn't have entered the business in the first place. But it is obviously important to consider all the relevant factors as carefully as you do in any other selling situation.

Promotion

In most companies, the obvious next step for a successful salesman is promotion to sales manager. Indeed, there is no reason why you should not aim higher still: many businesses are run by people who started in sales. But it may not necessarily be in your best interest to switch to management.

As many companies have discovered, the best salesman does not automatically make the best manager – just as a brilliant reporter does not necessarily make a brilliant editor. Investing the top producer with the trappings of

---

If you become a sales manager

Remember that motivation is crucial.

Be decisive: lead, don't follow.

Don't get bogged down in details: delegate.

Make sure that everyone understands what is expected of him, or her.

Don't set unrealistic targets.

Don't make threats unless you are prepared to act.

Be firm, but don't lose your temper.

Always remember what it was like to be one of the troops.

Be a good listener.

Be friendly, but never let them forget who is boss.

Discourage office politics: develop a team spirit.

Never forget to praise when it is merited.

Demand loyalty from the people who work for you – and be loyal to them.

Be as generous as you are allowed to be.

---

office does not immediately endow him with the talents required for managerial success.

Sales managers today face increasingly complex responsibilities. They must appreciate the multiplicity and the diversification of products, plus the heightened intricacies of marketing them. They must be able to interpret computer data as well as expense claims. And they must be able to get the best out of a *team*. The maverick salesman who is used to operating on his own, and looking after number one, often finds it hard to make the necessary transition. He hates being tied to an office desk, is reluctant to delegate and is bored with the administrative detail. The inevitable outcome is that both he and his superiors are unhappy. Sooner or later he is either fired or tries to find another job.

You really have to be quite honest with yourself. Most people come into sales because they enjoy the power of persuasion, because they get a kick out of each new customer conquest and because they are able to fill their day with people, not with paperwork. Why change all that? On the other hand, there is clearly much to be said for accepting a new challenge which tests your competitive drive. The supersalesman is not afraid of change; he welcomes it. He doesn't object to the shifts in attitude and habits required for competent performance.

You have to make up your own mind about this. There is no shame in being realistic in your ambitions and self-assessment. But there is no shame, either, in trying to reach for new heights. Look at the implications and make your choice. Don't say you will go into management unless you really mean it. If you decide to have a go, give it all you've got. The *next* step could lead you right into the Boardroom.

The First Million

There is nothing wrong with wanting to be a millionaire, whatever Socialists may say. The law rightly disapproves of people who get rich by selling cocaine and peddling fraudulent financial schemes, but the legitimate salesman has no reason to apologize for his ambitions.

Many people are in love with the idea of overnight success. The worker dreams about winning the pools or a mammoth lottery prize; the businessman hopes that, one day, he will pull off a hugely profitable deal. These things happen, of course, and the chances of making *real* money improve when one starts playing in the big league. As anyone who studies the financial pages knows, fortunes are being made every day. (They are also lost, but no one likes to advertise his failures.)

The supersalesman has a lot of opportunities which are denied to others, but if you work for a large corporation the scope is bound to be restricted. There are many people who make vast deals without any reward other than their salary. They are occasionally offered back-handers, but they know that accepting them will almost certainly cost them their jobs. The corporation executive is much more likely to make real money out of a share stake in his company or, at least, stock options. Even a comparatively modest holding can pay off handsomely if another corporation makes a take-over bid. If your company runs such a scheme, try to be part of it, even if it means foregoing an increase in salary.

But the most popular route to that elusive first million is

still the one I took myself. Launching a new business, alone or in association with others, calls for a lot of courage but it also has enticing possibilities. If you succeed, you have several pleasant choices. You can continue to build up the business (and pay yourself whatever salary you like), or sell a block of shares on the stock market for a fancy sum, or accept one of the offers which are sure to come along and spend the rest of your days in the sun. Many of today's multi-millionaires started as salesmen and later used the knowledge and contacts they acquired to become entrepreneurs.

Let me offer some rules, based not only on observation but also on my own experiences.

Do what you know best

It is surprising how often people fail because they go into fields they know nothing about. They are seduced by advertisements which offer attractive businesses for sale, and seldom stop to consider whether they are qualified to run them or why, if they are so lucrative, the present owners are eager to sell. A common error is to assume that one can run, say, a restaurant because one has been a customer for many years and watched the proprietor making money. A 100 per cent profit on a bottle of wine sounds like a good thing. One forgets about tedious details like rent, rates, lighting, heating, the cost of staff, wastage and all the evenings when the place is empty. The reality comes as a shock.

The people best placed to succeed are those who have spent a few years working for someone else in their chosen field. They at least know what they are up against. They know what it costs to get going, that established companies can be relied upon to defend their positions even if it means resorting to dirty tricks, that bad debts are an ever-present risk, and that business may fall off suddenly through no fault of their own.

I chose to go into magazine publishing because, after many years as financial editor of several daily newspapers, I had spent another ten years editing *Punch*. I was offered the *Punch* job, in 1969, because the old magazine was in a bad way and the proprietors thought I could bring it back to life. I worked very hard, doing just that. But ten years was long enough, and I was anxious to make some money. I very much doubt if I could have done it in any other type of business; besides, I wouldn't have had nearly as much fun in the process.

Choose the right associates

Mark McCormack, indisputably a supersalesman, thinks it's a mistake to take on partners. Some of the greatest entrepreneurial successes, he points out, have been solo acts.

This is certainly so, but I believe that some people *need* partners to prosper. Most small companies require an ideas man, a manager, a salesman and a first-class accountant. These qualities are seldom found rolled into one person, but they ought to be present in the company. I am primarily interested in writing, editing and developing new projects, which is a full-time job. I have no time, or desire, to manage an office or sell advertising, and I would make a terrible accountant. One can, of course, hire such people but there is a lot to be said for providing the right kind of motivation by giving them a stake in the business, as I did.

Mark also says that minority equity in a privately held corporation is 'worthless'. Again, I disagree. If someone makes a take-over bid, as they did in our case, *everyone* benefits.

Success is . . .

Here are some of my favourite quotes on the subject of success:

– Success isn't everything, but it makes a man stand straight.
Lillian Hellman

– One of the great advantages of success is that you don't have to listen to good advice any more.
Bernard Buffet

– Success is simply a matter of luck. Ask any failure.
Earl Wilson

– The compensation of a very early success is a conviction that life is a romantic matter. In the best sense one stays young.
F. Scott Fitzgerald

– The way to secure success is to be more anxious about obtaining it than about deserving it.
William Hazlitt

— When men succeed, even their neighbours think them wise.

Pindar

— If A equals success, then the formula is $A = X + Y - Z$. X is work, Y is play, Z is keep your mouth shut.

Albert Einstein

— Contrary to the cliche, genuinely nice guys most often finish first, or very near it.

Malcolm Forbes

— Success often comes from taking a misstep in the right direction.

Anonymous

— Successful people are the ones who can think up things for the rest of the world to keep busy at.

Don Marquis

— Success is the ability to get along with some people and ahead of others.

Anonymous

— The toughest thing about being a success is that you've got to keep on being a success.

Irving Berlin

— Failures makes a man bitter and cruel. Success improves the character of the man.

W. Somerset Maugham

Aim High

Many ideas fail to make millions because they have limited scope or because the people behind them lack the courage to go for vigorous expansion. It is vital to concentrate on projects which offer a chance of substantial growth. Ask yourself: how large could this company be a decade from now?

Having chosen the right business, you must think big. The ambitious caterer is not satisfied with opening one restaurant: like Ray Kroc, he wants to build a chain. The enterprising retailer may start with one shop but his aim is to acquire many more.

Once you get under way, you must not allow yourself to get bogged down. You have to believe (as every true supersalesman does) that you can achieve just about anything if you really try. If you want to be super-rich, you can't afford to have the attitude of a small-time grocer.

Finance is easier to come by once you have a successful track record. Never be afraid to borrow – most fortunes are made by using OPM, Other People's Money. Few of the big names in the business world today had large amounts of cash when they embarked on their bold ventures. Indeed, some of them are still deeply in debt.

It is a banker's job to lend money to the 'right' people: he would soon go out of business if he spent all his time saying no. But banks are by no means the only source. Pension funds and insurance companies have staggering sums at their disposal, and are generally willing to consider any proposition which seems likely to give them a good return.

One of the most interesting developments in recent years has been the management buy-out. Put simply, this is a transaction whereby the managers of a business join with financial institutions to buy that business from its present owners. The institutions put up most of the money in the form of debt and loan stock, and take part of the equity. The managers put all the cash they can raise into equity and run the business.

Don't be a one-product firm

It is always dangerous, in business, to tie one's fortunes to a single product, however good it may be. When rivals hit back, as they inevitably do, you may be left high and dry. Advertising agencies don't rely on one client; nor do I. There's safety in numbers – and that applies as much to a company supplying, say, components as it does to a magazine publisher.

Plan ahead

The biggest test, I have found, comes when you have had some success and are not quite sure what to do next. Many people are so busy coping with what they have built that they don't have time to think about the future. They ought to be launching new products, but they simply can't get around to it. I believe that I have found the answer. Go off to the Caribbean for a month (preferably in December or January) and leave your colleagues to get on with it.

The Second Million

It is generally easier to make the second million than the first. You have shown what you can do, and you have assets which can be used as security for loans. People have greater faith in you and will probably be eager to get in on your act. This 'take-off effect' is a well-known phenomenon.

Only you can decide whether you want to go *on* making millions. Many self-made people work just as hard after they have passed that magic million mark as they did before. They don't want to stop (or perhaps don't know how to stop) because they enjoy the power and prestige that comes with success. Money as such ceases to be all-important; it is merely the yardstick by which the world judges their success. Rupert Murdoch doesn't *need* another fortune. Nor does Robert Maxwell. They are turned on by the thrill of the chase, the joy of winning. They don't dream of a leisurely life on some Caribbean beach: it would bore them to tears. You may be like them – many supersalesmen are – or you may feel that money should be the means to an entirely different end: travel, plenty of time for golf or some other hobby, more time with the family. It's nice, you will agree, to be in a position to choose.

When the Headhunter Calls

Being wooed by a headhunter is good for the ego: it confirms that you have arrived. Your name is known; others have discussed your success; important people think you would be a tremendous asset.

The courtship ritual usually starts with a discreet phone call. He has been asked to find a top salesman/manager/ executive/managing director. Are you free to talk? Do you know anyone who might be suitable? Would you, by any chance, be interested yourself? You would? That's marvellous.

What you don't know, of course, is that he has already talked to several other people. His client expects him to produce a short-list (that's how he earns his exorbitant fee) and he is not going to make you an offer there and then. Indeed, you may never get an offer at all. The client may meet you over lunch and decide that you are not the person he wants. He will, however, question you closely about your company's activities and your own role – as far as he is concerned, the lunch won't be wasted if he finds out what his competitor is up to.

Be careful what you say – it may get back to your employers. And don't be too eager. The way to handle a headhunter – and the people he works for – is to indicate that you *might*, just might, be interested in making a move. Ask some searching questions of your own. What happened to the man you are supposed to replace? Was he promoted? Was he fired? Is this a new position? If so, why was it created? Remember that he is not working for you, but for the people who pay him. If they are really keen to have you, they will have done their homework and will gladly meet your terms. Don't be afraid to name an outrageous price. The worst thing that can happen is that you will have to stay where you are. Sooner or later you will get another call . . .

Quiz: Have You Got What It Takes?

Have You Got What It Takes?

Test your qualification for supersalesman status by answering this simple quiz. Be honest. Then turn to page . . . 201 . . . and check your score.

1 Do you agree with the following statements?
(a) You cannot do business on social occasions.
(b) If you want something done right, you must do it yourself.
(c) Recessions are periods of opportunity.
(d) Success is simply a matter of luck.

2 How do you feel about rejection? Do you:
(a) Take it personally?
(b) Shrug your shoulders and move on to the next deal?
(c) Try to discover the reason and learn from the experience?
(d) See it as a challenge, and try to change the prospect's mind?

3 Review the way you manage your time, and give honest answers to these questions.
(a) Do you set yourself definite goals?
(b) Do you worry a lot about details?
(c) Are you good at delegating?
(d) Do you set yourself deadlines?

4 A prospect has failed to respond to your calls and letters. Would you:
(a) Give up?
(b) Write to his superiors, complaining about his lack of courtesy?
(c) Seek an opportunity to meet him socially?
(d) Try to find out his home telephone number and address, and contact him there?

5 You are asked to present your case to a group of executives. Would you:
(a) Read out a standard written presentation, incorporating as much detail as possible?
(b) Stick to essentials and use plenty of audio-visual aids?
(c) Encourage them to comment on your proposals as you go along?
(d) Stress how important the deal is to you and your company?

6 You have made a good presentation, but the prospect is still undecided. Would you:
(a) Ask for the order?
(b) Give him more time?
(c) Go over it all again?
(d) Apply forceful pressure?

7 The prospect comes up with an objection which strikes you as unreasonable. Would you:
(a) Ignore it?
(b) Point out how wrong he is?
(c) Ask him to elaborate?
(d) Get him to suggest a remedy?

8 The prospect has made a commitment to buy. Do you:
(a) Praise him warmly for making the right decision?
(b) Settle all the details there and then?

(c) Say nothing, and leave as soon as you can?

(d) Switch the conversation to some other topic, such as the weather?

9 You are offered an opportunity to do a deal which is bigger than anything you have ever handled before. Would you:

(a) Agree at once?

(b) Admit that it is out of your range?

(c) Promise to look into it?

(d) Pass it on to someone with more experience?

10 How do you feel about change? Do you:

(a) Resent it?

(b) Welcome it?

(c) Learn to live with it, however irritating it may be?

(d) Try to lead the way?

11 You are offered another job which carries higher risks but which also holds out the prospect of much bigger rewards. Would you:

(a) Decline with thanks?

(b) Accept with alacrity?

(c) Use the offer to squeeze more money and/or promotion out of your present employers?

(d) Ask for time to consider what you would be letting yourself in for?

12 You find yourself sitting next to the head of a large corporation on a flight to New York and embark on a conversation. Do you:

(a) Tell him your life story?

(b) Try to interest him in your product or service?

(c) Encourage him to talk about his work?

(d) Forget all about it the moment you land?

13 You have a meeting with an Arab oil millionaire who seems reluctant to get down to business. Do you:
(a) Tell him about your marvellous proposition and hand over your company's sales literature?
(b) Remind him that you have a plane to catch?
(c) Wait for him to raise the subject?
(d) Come back another time?

14 Looking ahead, which of these options has most appeal for you?
(a) Promotion to senior management level.
(b) Making a million.
(c) Steady employment and a reasonable income when you retire.
(d) Starting your own business.

Now run your eye down these columns and total up your score.

1	(a) 1	(b) 1	(c) 4	(d) 0
2	(a) 0	(b) 2	(c) 4	(d) 4
3	(a) 4	(b) 1	(c) 4	(d) 4
4	(a) 1	(b) 0	(c) 3	(d) 2
5	(a) 1	(b) 4	(c) 3	(d) 0
6	(a) 4	(b) 1	(c) 1	(d) 0
7	(a) 1	(b) 0	(c) 4	(d) 4
8	(a) 1	(b) 1	(c) 3	(d) 3
9	(a) 2	(b) 1	(c) 4	(d) 2
10	(a) 0	(b) 4	(c) 3	(d) 4
11	(a) 1	(b) 3	(c) 2	(d) 4
12	(a) 1	(b) 4	(c) 3	(d) 0
13	(a) 1	(b) 0	(c) 4	(d) 3
14	(a) 3	(b) 4	(c) 1	(d) 3

Evaluating your Score

If you scored between 48 and 56
Congratulations: if you are not a supersalesman already, you have what it takes to get to the top.

Between 40–47
Not bad. Read this book again and see how you can do better.

Between 30–39
You are probably a very nice person, but you seem to lack the determination needed to become something special in the world of selling. You're Number three: try harder.

Between 10 and 29
Oh, dear. Unless you make a big effort to catch up, you are likely to be stuck on the lower rungs of the ladder. Perhaps you should consider some other line of business?

Bestselling Non-Fiction

☐ The Alexander Principle	Wilfred Barlow	£2.95
☐ The Complete Book of Exercises	Diagram Group	£4.95
☐ Everything is Negotiable	Gavin Kennedy	£2.95
☐ Health on Your Plate	Janet Pleshette	£2.50
☐ The Cheiro Book of Fate and Fortune	Cheiro	£2.95
☐ The Handbook of Chinese Horoscopes	Theodora Lau	£2.50
☐ Hollywood Babylon	Kenneth Anger	£7.95
☐ Hollywood Babylon II	Kenneth Anger	£7.95
☐ The Domesday Heritage	Ed. Elizabeth Hallam	£3.95
☐ Historic Railway Disasters	O. S. Nock	£2.50
☐ Wildlife of the Domestic Cat	Roger Tabor	£4.50
☐ Elvis and Me	Priscilla Presley	£2.95
☐ Maria Callas	Arianna Stassinopoulos	£2.50
☐ The Brendan Voyage	Tim Severin	£3.50

Bestselling Non-Fiction

☐ The Gradual Vegetarian	Lisa Tracy	£2.95
☐ The Food Scandal	Caroline Walker & Geoffrey Cannon	£3.95
☐ Harmony Rules	Gary Butt & Frena Bloomfield	£2.25
☐ Everything is Negotiable	Gavin Kennedy	£2.95
☐ Hollywood Babylon	Kevin Anger	£7.95
☐ Red Watch	Gordon Honeycombe	£2.75
☐ Wildlife of the Domestic Cat	Roger Tabor	£4.50
☐ The World of Placido Domingo	Daniel Snowman	£4.95
☐ The Sinbad Voyage	Tim Severin	£2.75
☐ The Hills is Lonely	Lillian Beckwith	£1.95
☐ English Country Cottage	R. J. Brown	£3.50
☐ Raw Energy	Leslie & Susannah Kenton	£2.95

ARROW BOOKS, BOOKSERVICE BY POST, PO BOX 29, DOUGLAS, ISLE OF MAN, BRITISH ISLES

NAME ....

ADDRESS ....

....

....

Please enclose a cheque or postal order made out to Arrow Books Ltd. for the amount due and allow the following for postage and packing.

U.K. CUSTOMERS: Please allow 22p per book to a maximum of £3.00.

B.F.P.O. & EIRE: Please allow 22p per book to a maximum of £3.00.

OVERSEAS CUSTOMERS: Please allow 22p per book.

Whilst every effort is made to keep prices low it is sometimes necessary to increase cover prices at short notice. Arrow Books reserve the right to show new retail prices on covers which may differ from those previously advertised in the text or elsewhere.

Bestselling War Fiction and Non-Fiction

- [ ] Passage to Mutiny — Alexander Kent — £2.50
- [ ] The Flag Captain — Alexander Kent — £2.50
- [ ] Badge of Glory — Douglas Reeman — £2.50
- [ ] Winged Escort — Douglas Reeman — £2.50
- [ ] Army of Shadows — John Harris — £2.50
- [ ] Up for Grabs — John Harris — £2.50
- [ ] Decoy — Dudley Pope — £1.95
- [ ] Curse of the Death's Head — Rupert Butler — £2.25
- [ ] Gestapo — Rupert Butler — £2.75
- [ ] Auschwitz and the Allies — Martin Gilbert — £4.95
- [ ] Tumult in the Clouds — James A. Goodson — £2.95
- [ ] Sigh for a Merlin — Alex Henshaw — £2.50
- [ ] Morning Glory — Stephen Howarth — £4.95
- [ ] The Doodlebugs — Norman Longmate — £4.95
- [ ] Colditz – The Full Story — Major P. Reid — £2.95

ARROW BOOKS, BOOKSERVICE BY POST, PO BOX 29, DOUGLAS, ISLE OF MAN, BRITISH ISLES

NAME ....

ADDRESS ....

....

....

Please enclose a cheque or postal order made out to Arrow Books Ltd. for the amount due and allow the following for postage and packing.

U.K. CUSTOMERS: Please allow 22p per book to a maximum of £3.00.

B.F.P.O. & EIRE: Please allow 22p per book to a maximum of £3.00.

OVERSEAS CUSTOMERS: Please allow 22p per book.

Whilst every effort is made to keep prices low it is sometimes necessary to increase cover prices at short notice. Arrow Books reserve the right to show new retail prices on covers which may differ from those previously advertised in the text or elsewhere.

A Selection of Arrow Bestsellers

☐ Voices on the Wind	Evelyn Anthony	£2.50
☐ Someone Else's Money	Michael M. Thomas	£2.50
☐ The Executioner's Song	Norman Mailer	£3.50
☐ The Alexander Principle	Wilfred Barlow	£2.95
☐ Everything is Negotiable	Gavin Kennedy	£2.95
☐ The New Girlfriend & other stories	Ruth Rendell	£1.95
☐ An Unkindness of Ravens	Ruth Rendell	£1.95
☐ Dead in the Morning	Margaret Yorke	£1.75
☐ The Domesday Heritage	Ed. Elizabeth Hallam	£3.95
☐ Elvis and Me	Priscilla Presley	£2.95
☐ The World of Placido Domingo	Daniel Snowman	£4.95
☐ Maria Callas	Arianna Stassinopoulos	£2.50
☐ The Brendan Voyage	Tim Severin	£3.50
☐ A Shine of Rainbows	Lillian Beckwith	£1.95
☐ Rates of Exchange	Malcolm Bradbury	£2.95
☐ Thy Tears Might Cease	Michael Farrell	£2.95
☐ Pudding and Pie (Nancy Mitford Omnibus)	Nancy Mitford	£3.95

ARROW BOOKS, BOOKSERVICE BY POST, PO BOX 29, DOUGLAS, ISLE OF MAN, BRITISH ISLES

NAME ....

ADDRESS ....

....

....

Please enclose a cheque or postal order made out to Arrow Books Ltd. for the amount due and allow the following for postage and packing.

U.K. CUSTOMERS: Please allow 22p per book to a maximum of £3.00.

B.F.P.O. & EIRE: Please allow 22p per book to a maximum of £3.00.

OVERSEAS CUSTOMERS: Please allow 22p per book.

Whilst every effort is made to keep prices low it is sometimes necessary to increase cover prices at short notice. Arrow Books reserve the right to show new retail prices on covers which may differ from those previously advertised in the text or elsewhere.